REIKI HEALING

FOR BEGINNERS

A Practical Guide to Learning the Fundamentals
of Reiki Healing for Common Ailments

By Abigail Welsh

REIKI HEALING

© Copyright 2020 - All rights reserved.

The content contained within this book may not be reproduced, duplicated or transmitted without direct written permission from the author or the publisher.

Under no circumstances will any blame or legal responsibility be held against the publisher, or author, for any damages, reparation, or monetary loss due to the information contained within this book. Either directly or indirectly.

Legal Notice:

This book is copyright protected. This book is only for personal use. You cannot amend, distribute, sell, use, quote or paraphrase any part, or the content within this book, without the consent of the author or publisher.

Disclaimer Notice:

Please note the information contained within this document is for educational and entertainment purposes only. All effort has been executed to present accurate, up to date, and reliable, complete information. No warranties of any kind are declared or implied. Readers acknowledge that the author is not engaging in the rendering of legal, financial, medical or professional advice. The content within this book has been derived from various sources. Please consult a licensed professional before attempting any techniques outlined in this book.

By reading this document, the reader agrees that under no circumstances is the author responsible for any losses, direct or indirect, which are incurred as a result of the use of information contained within this document, including, but not limited to, — errors, omissions, or inaccuracies.

Table of Contents

Introduction vi

Chapter One - The History Of Reiki 1

   The Reiki Masters And The Spread Of The Practice Globally 8

Chapter Two - Health Benefits 15

   Find Balance 17

   Deep Relaxation 19

   Remove Energy Blockages 22

   Clear The Mind 24

   Promote Better Sleep 27

   Improve Spiritual Growth 30

   Help To Improve Mood 33

Chapter Three - Types Of Reiki 40

   Usui Reiki 42

   Jikiden Reiki 46

   Karuna Reiki 49

   Lightarian Reiki 54

   Seichim Reiki 56

Chapter Four - A Typical Reiki Session 63

   The Typical Reiki Setting 65

How Long Does A Reiki Session Last?......................68

What Happens During A Reiki Session? 72

What Do You Experience During A Typical Reiki Session?..75

What You Should Do During And After A Reiki Session 82

Chapter Five - Reiki Techniques 91

A Crash Course On Reiki Training...........................93

Healing Yourself With Reiki....................................106

Reiki Hand Positions 112

Chapter Six - Reiki For Common Ailments 125

Headaches 125

Backaches..127

Arthritis...128

High Blood Pressure 129

Eczema 130

Chapter Seven - The Three Degrees Of Reiki.......... 135

First Degree - Shoden 136

Second Degree - Okuden 137

Third Degree - Shinpiden......................................139

Final Words.. 142

INTRODUCTION

The topic of reiki healing has been a complicated one. Reiki is often looked at as a pseudoscience, a fake practice which has conned hundreds of thousands of people since its invention in 1922. Many scientifically-minded people have gone to bat to destabilize and discredit this practice. Yet the many people both practicing and receiving reiki care have sworn to the palpable energy they feel during the practice as well as the benefits it has brought into their life.

Deciding whether or not reiki is worth experiencing has to be an individual process, one in which even someone like myself cannot sway your opinion. If you have set it in your mind that reiki is fake then you are going to find that any experience you have with the practice aligns with this mindset. When we approach the realm of the spiritual, that immaterial plane in which we shape our reality, what we choose to believe brings great power. When we choose to believe something is fake, we experience it as fake. But when we make the choice to believe in the possibilities for wellness that are offered by a practice like reiki, we find that the benefits flow into our life like a mighty river.

The world of the spiritual, of the divine, of the great elemental energy around us all, is a world that people have been exploring for centuries and centuries. For as long as we have been exploring it, there have been those who would disregard it with the swipe of a hand. If you find yourself reading this book and feeling that way then you can be sure that the mindset you have cultivated is not one fit to plant the seeds of reiki in, nor other spirituality healing techniques, either. Those who are willing to plant the seeds and water the garden of their own innate energy will find much of value within themselves and within the pages of this book you now hold in your hands.

This book is going to dive deep into the practice of reiki to help you understand it and the value it can bring into your life. To begin, we will be looking at the history of reiki in Chapter One. There are practitioners who try to claim that reiki is an ancient technique; its origins date back to the early 1900s. This attempt to situate reiki into a false narrative of an ancient, grand tradition truly does a disservice to its roots. Rather than inflate the history of the practice, we will look at it as it truly was. Viewing reiki through the lens of its authentic historical development is important because when people overblow and inflate reality it only gives more ammunition to those who are looking to tear it down.

With the history out of the way, Chapter Two moves us into a discussion of the health benefits that are associated with reiki. These benefits range from a reduction of stress to a reduction of the negative effects of depression; an increase in true relaxation; an improved quality of life; and even more peaceful, less turbulent sleep. It is important to realize that the benefits of reiki are first and foremost achieved on a spiritual and mental level rather than a physical level. There are some physical benefits which reiki brings but this is another area in which it is often overblown. In fact, there are some people who claim to be practitioners of reiki that argue it can be as beneficial as to cure cancer. These are outlandish claims which only serve to weaken the opinion of reiki in the eyes of the public. It is not a miracle cure for everything that ails you like some people claim.

Chapter Three will look at the different types of reiki: usui, karun and lightarian. These will help to give a sense of how the different schools of reiki practice differ from one another. This conversation will flow naturally into Chapter Four where we look at a typical reiki session in action. Where the session takes place, how long it lasts, what actually happens during it, what experience you can expect and what actions you are to take during will all be discussed at length. This chapter will then flow into Chapter Five where we highlight the different techniques used in reiki. These three chapters will work together to form the core of our reiki knowledge and help you to reach the energy trapped inside of yourself.

In Chapter Six, we will discuss the way that reiki can be used to help with common ailments. Problems like headaches and backaches, arthritis and eczema and even high blood pressure can benefit from reiki treatments. Notice, however, that these are simple and common ailments rather than complex ones such as cancer or diabetes. These common ailments can also be causes in and of themselves or they can be caused by other underlying issues. Reiki is not a technique that should ever replace your doctor's medical advice. The best benefits come from mixing your spiritual healing, like reiki, together with the knowledge from the medical community. For example, a combination of Advil and reiki practice can completely clear up a headache where the painkiller and the reiki alone would only help to shrink it down rather than dissolve it. In going through this book, please consider reiki to be a supplementary practice rather than a replacement.

This goes beyond just the medical realm and enters into the spiritual, as well. Reiki is a spiritual healing technique but if your spiritual energy is out of whack then how could you expect reiki to work? Practices for the spirit such as meditation or prayer are incredibly important. Reiki doesn't give you a spiritual practice but rather it is a way of shaping and using your spiritual energy to improve your life and the life of those around you. If you don't already have a spiritual practice then I want to strongly recommend that you start meditating before you try these techniques. The deeper the connection you have to your own spiritual energy, the better you will find your results with reiki to be.

We'll be closing out the book with Chapter Seven and a discussion on the different levels of reiki. Reiki is broken up into degrees. The first degree is the shoden and it represents the introductory level of reiki. This is where you will be by the end of the book. You won't, however, just be at the beginning of the level; you'll be well on your way towards the second degree, okuden. This is the level at which most people can be considered a practitioner of reiki. If you are looking to practice rather than receive then you will be working your way towards okuden. The practical knowledge in this book will help you on this journey but you must work hard to get there. The final degree is called shinpiden and it is the level at which you are considered to be a master. It will take you a long, long time to get to this point. It will take a lot of practice and a lot of learning to reach the degree of shinpiden.

May you find the journey there to be a peaceful one.

Let us begin.

CHAPTER ONE

THE HISTORY OF REIKI

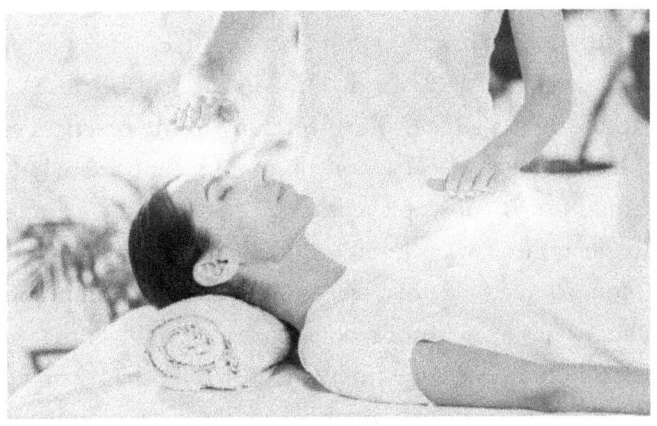

Reiki is a fascinating topic, one which has proven captivating to hundreds of thousands of people. In this chapter it is my goal to lay out the history of reiki in as straightforward and honest of a way as possible. To do so we will be limiting ourselves to reiki as founded by Mikao Usui. One of the first points of contention that this book will make is to point out that while he is often known as Dr. Mikao Usui, the fact of the matter is that Usui never earned a doctorate or had a formal education in medicine as we understand that formal education today.

Usui nevertheless had a very enlightened and enlightening education and life, one that has continued to provide value to the world long since his death. He was not a doctor by our modern standards. Please understand that I mean the man no harm but rather want to situate him firmly within historical fact. He is often referred to as Dr. Usui or Dr. Mikao Usui because he had brought a large body of teaching to the practices of holistic medicine. His contribution is important and should not be downplayed. One of the aspects of reiki that its critics always jump on is the fact that Usui wasn't a doctor. We will not give the critics any ammunition. Stating that Usui is not a doctor, despite the fact that he has this title, is an argument against reiki that distracts and detracts from the larger discussion by narrowing in on the minor details.

As mentioned in the introduction, reiki practitioners often report the historical significance of reiki with a level of exaggeration which I believe is actually harmful to the practice. Anything that over-inflates reiki can be harmful to reiki because it gives those critics another foothold in decry and defame this practice. This approach is often upsetting to those that have bought into (or, even helped to fuel) the mysterious and 'ancient' lore. To hear someone say that Mikao Usui was not a doctor is downright offensive to some. If reiki is to ever gain the respect and reputation that it deserves then such statements need to be said, highlighted and shared.

Making such statements don't need to be viewed as a disservice when describing the enlightened and benevolent man that Usui was. I hope that you, dear reader, can see that what I am attempting to do is honor the man as he was. Honor his practice as it is. To do so is to give Usui and reiki the grounding it so often lacks when it comes to discussions of the practice.

With that said, let us now meet Mikao Usui and see how reiki came to be, how it spread across continents and came to be settled in North America as well as Asia.

Mikao Usui, a Buddhist Upbringing and the Foundation of Reiki

Reiki begins with Mikao Usui. His discovery of the techniques helped to change the world. While the introduction of reiki is not until 1922 and the founding of the first reiki clinic, the root of the practice does run much deeper. This does not mean that reiki is an ancient technique but rather that it is a technique that is founded on concepts that have been around for centuries. Ideas such as the body's natural system of energy and the way that the individual balances these energies are integral to the formation of reiki. These practices do have a long and storied history; reiki is one of the newer incarnations of these techniques or integrating the relationships connected to them.

It should not be surprising to find that reiki draws inspiration from traditional beliefs, especially those of a buddhist nature. Usui was fortunate to be born into a wealthy buddhist family in the middle of the 19th Century. This provided Usui with opportunities that would have been beyond the capabilities of many living at the time. His family's wealth meant that they could afford to privilege their son with a full education at a point in time where most individuals were granted a rudimentary education at best. This had the effect of triggering a life-long interest into the realm of the investigative and intellectual. This desire, this need to know how things worked and to take apart systems of knowledge would stick with Usui throughout the whole of his life.

The wealth of knowledge that his parent's wealth brought him was only one half of the story. Just as important was the fact that his family were devout buddhists. Usui began training at buddhist monasteries while he was quite young, evidently he was still a child as he was being taught the way of the samurai. Swordsmanship, Kiko (which is the Japanese form of Qigong) and martial arts were all among Usui's training. While this samurai education came at a point in which the Japanese were moving away from the old traditions, they would prove to be extremely important to how Usui saw the world and to how he discovered his path towards healing.

This education was first and foremost one of a buddhist upbringing but buddhism has always been quite inclusive in the scope of its teachings. A strong element of any healthy buddhist training is to look at the other religions through which buddhism must, by nature, interact. Alongside his more formal education, this fuelled an interest in theology, as well as in the mind and the body. These latter two subjects would find purchase in Usui's interests in the study of psychology and medicine. With these three key pathways in front of him, Usui would need to decide which way to focus his attention. In the beginning, his energies were most strongly focused on his buddhist ideals but the other two interests weren't to be forgotten.

Usui travelled a lot in his life. He would roam the world and learn about the systems of healing he discovered. One of the important things to understand is that while he was a buddhst, eventually becoming a buddhist priest who lived in a monastery, he kept himself open to the possibilities and the lessons inherent in the healing systems he was studying. It didn't matter whether or not he believed in them fully. Instead, what mattered was that he gave them a fair and honest appraisal and he often made an effort to seek them out in practice so that he could bear witness. Among his travels, prior to becoming a buddhist priest proper, he worked in the role of a reporter, a missionary, a secretary. He even spent time serving as a guard and another as a public servant. Wherever Usui went, he made sure to find work as he still needed shelter and food, but whenever possible he made it a priority to work in areas that benefited the larger population.

Training to be a buddhist monk was an experience of profound significance. In the history of Islam, the prophet Muhammad discovered the divine while meditating in a cave. Buddhism was brought to the public by the Buddha after a long period of meditating at the base of a tree. Part of Usui's training was to fast, meditate and pray in a cave on the side of Mount Kurama just north of the Japanese city of Kyoto. Usui maintained this practice for twenty days, experiencing a deep sense of connection between no-self and the world around him. No-self is a concept in Buddhism in which believers practice a meditation of letting go of the idea of self and expanding their awareness throughout as much of creation as they can. It was deep in this practice that Usui would have his revelation on the twenty-first day.

On that fateful twenty-first day, Usui had a revelation. As he meditated in the darkened cave he began to see Sanskrit symbols. These symbols revealed to him the interwoven nature of the many healing practices he had studied around the world and it was through these interconnections that he discovered reiki. It's worth making a quick note about the Sanskrit he saw. Usui was a Japanese man but Buddhism finds its roots in India and many of the key words used in buddhist teaching are in Sanskrit. What Usui was seeing in that cave harkened back to the very foundation and formulation of the religion he had studied since he was a boy.

So what did Usui do with this learning? First thing to do was to come down from the mountain and to begin capturing what he experienced. The next step was to open up his teachings and share them with the public. To achieve this he opened the first reiki clinic that the world had ever seen. The location of Kyoto was always within view of the mountain from which he brought back his knowledge. Usui wasn't satisfied with simply performing this practice. If he was, then surely it would have disappeared into nothing more than a footnote in the long and storied history of Japanese Buddhism. Usui believed in the beneficial effects of reiki and he wanted to ensure that it continued in the world after he was gone.

To achieve this, Usui didn't just open a clinic. He opened a reiki school and began to teach. From its opening in 1922 until his death in 1926, Usui spent his time teaching a generation of reiki masters who would take this practice and spread it overseas.

The Reiki Masters and the Spread of the Practice Globally

One of the most well known reiki masters that Usui trained was Chujiro Hayashi. Having served as a naval officer, Hayashi took a strong interest in reiki and was found to be naturally gifted. Of course, that natural gift meant nothing without the training and discipline that Usui instilled in him. Hayashi set up the second reiki clinic, this one further to the east in Tokyo.

Hayashi continued the development of what is called the Usui system of reiki. We'll spend Chapter Three looking at the differences between the various systems of reiki that are still extant today. Hayashi added a range of hand positions to the Usui system so that it could better cover the body. As reiki is about the working of energy through the palms, being able to cover the body in full alignment is extremely important. Usui was still developing the system when he passed away and so it was left up to the masters he trained to complete his work.

Hayashi was responsible for another change in the reiki system. There is a process which we call attunement and it is through attunement that the teacher hands over power to the student. The first level of attunement is achieved by opening the crown, heart and palm chakras and creating a link (the attunement) between the student and the source of the energy. Hayashi helped to develop this attunement process to make it easier for the student. This helped Hayashi in training further students to be reiki masters but it has had a detrimental effect as well. The problem here is that in simplifying the process, it has made it easier for people to pretend to be masters or to pretend to be capable of training. Some of these individuals may even believe it in their heart of hearts that they are masters but they built this belief on what buddhists would refer to as a false premise.

A false premise is easier to spot in another. Say a wife meets with a friend when her husband is gone. She is in discussions about how to bring joy into her husband's life through a surprise present and is enlisting a friend to help her keep it a surprise. The husband, upon coming home early, sees the friend leaving and questions his wife about it. The wife will not say what the purpose of the visit was and so the husband grows suspicious that his wife is having an affair. To confirm his suspicions the husband decides to skip work and watch his house from a hidden location. Seeing the friend return, he convinces himself that his suspicions were right and he starts to plan how to get back at his wife. In the husband's mind, he fully believes himself to have a knowledge that he does not. He believes he sees reality for what it is but his perception is a false premise. Just like the husband in this story fails to see reality for what it is, there are "reiki" practitioners who aren't actually practicing reiki. They have not received attunement properly and so they are deluding themselves. This is an unfortunate side-effect of Chujuiro Hayashi's redefinition of the attunement process.

Hayashi did train other masters, though, including an extremely important woman by the name of Hawayo Takata. Takata met with Hayashi for healing and became so interested in reiki that she became one of his most valuable students. If that was the end of her story, we wouldn't be mentioning it but Takata had an important feature that set her apart from the other masters. Those trained by Usui and Hayashi were all of Japanese descent, except for Mrs. Takata. Takata was a Japanese-American woman who lived in the States most of the time. She attended her training in Tokyo but when she was finished she returned to the United States, bringing reiki with her.

When Takata returned home to the States, she had been at level two. This means that she was not a master at the time. She kept on studying, however, and practicing reiki and was said to have become a master. Much like Hayashi did, Takata also made changes to the practice. At this point, the practice had changed not once but twice as it came to be introduced to America. It was this changed version of reiki that is most commonly practiced in North America; Takata trained twenty-two masters before she passed away.

Different forms of reiki have developed in the ninety-eight years since Usui opened that first clinic in

Kyoto. Each style has its own teachers and practitioners but I have found that I trust these newer practitioners far less than I do those that have continued to practice Usui reiki. Mikao Usui stole fire from the gods within that cave of his and the further we have moved away from his teachings, the harder it has been to show the positive side of reiki. As we go forward in this book, we aim at connecting back to these early stages of practice and the universal energy it involves.

Chapter Summary

- Reiki is a form of palm healing. Practitioners are opened up to the healing energies of reiki through an attunement process and they use this to heal.

- There are a lot of confusing facts floating around about the founder of reiki, Mikao Usui. These only serve to give opponents of this practice room to attack it.

- Mikao Usui was raised as a buddhist and a scholar. He was able to attend religious training early in life and he travelled around, learning about alternative forms of medicine.

- Usui was meditating in a cave for several days when he suddenly had an extremely spiritual encounter and the power of reiki was revealed to him.

- Usui took reiki back to the people of Japan and opened up the first ever reiki clinic in 1922.

- From 1922 until his death in 1926, Usui spent his time healing patients and training the first ever generation of reiki masters.

- One master that Usui trained was Chujiro Hayashi. Hayashi opened up the second ever reiki clinic and continued the development of the process after Usui's death.

- Hayashi trained a woman by the name of Hawayo Takata. Takata was a Japanese-American and she brought reiki to North America after reaching the second degree.

- Takata made changes to the practice and trained twenty-two "masters" in North America. The second degree of reiki is often referred to as "Western reiki" because there were no true "masters" in North America like there were in Japan.

- There are many more types of reiki in the world today than 98 years ago when it invented but they all trace their roots to the discoveries and teachings of Usui.

In the next chapter, you will learn about the various benefits of reiki healing. These range from a deep sense of relaxation to an improvement in your sleep. It can help you to break down your stress and pump up the quality of your life. To learn more about these and more, flip to the next page and dive into Chapter Two.

CHAPTER TWO

HEALTH BENEFITS

Those who practice reiki through false premise claim that it is the end-all, be-all of healing techniques. You will see reiki recommended for cancer patients, diabetics and even those who are dealing with erectile dysfunction. The truth of the matter is that many of today's practitioners don't have the power to provide you any of the benefits, let alone such profound ones.

If you are considering reiki for health benefits or illnesses that are life-threatening then, please, make sure that you combine it with Western medicine to achieve the benefits of both Eastern and Western practices. I would recommend this even to those who are meeting with long-term, experienced masters. It is always best to combine benefits rather than detract from them. Reiki shouldn't be seen as an alternative to Western medicine but rather as an addition.

The benefits that we are looking at in this chapter are those that most readily pop up. Even a practitioner who is working from a false premise can achieve a few of these effects, though not to nearly the same level that a true master can. Even when achieving an effect, such as stress reduction, the difference you feel between a true master and a practitioner working from a false premise is palpable. If you are dealing with stress in one area, reiki may help you to deal with it but the high blood pressure caused by your stress might benefit best from medication prescribed by a doctor. The doctor helps you to reduce the blood pressure while the reiki helps you to let go of the vibrational blockages that created the blood pressure rising stress in the first place.

Together, we can see reiki and Western medicine as holding hands. When we view these practices in this way we truly open ourselves up to the best possible life we can have.

Find Balance

One of the biggest challenges facing humankind these days is a lack of balance and harmony. The modern day and age has moved away from the more spiritually connected existence that humans have lived for most of our history. We used to have a much deeper connection to the world around us, one that helped to keep us rooted in the present moment. Research has shown that meditation and mindfulness provide a wide range of benefits to us.

With our smartphones and 24-hour news cycle, social media and non-stop emails, is it any surprise that many of us have lost the sense of balance that we had? How can it be shocking to find that we lack a sense of harmony when we're always being pulled a thousand directions at once. This constant interconnectivity seems wonderful on the surface and I will be the first to admit that it has brought a lot of positive change into the world. We have mistaken internet connection with the deeper, more fulfilling connection to the world around us.

Reiki healing is one of the ways that we can help to restore this balance. We must first take the time out of our busy schedules to book our appointments and then come in. Right away this is offering a benefit: it is helping us to step away from the repetitive cycles we all experience every day and it is placing us into a space (mentally) in which we are already more open, more receptive to the healing energies of the universe. As these healing energies are worked through your body, you will find a deep sense of relaxation, which we talk about in a moment. More than the relaxation itself, balance is found by taking the time to get away from everything.

Too many people reach for drugs or alcohol to help them deal with the mundanity and struggle of everyday life. These approaches only help to further distort our sense of harmony and balance. If you reach for alcohol when you are stressed then you start to reach for it every time and you build a false perception in which you will only be happy if you have the substance. In this example drinking is done to help the self but it only distorts it. Reiki, along with practices like meditation and yoga, is a much better, much healthier way of finding balance. The balance you take from practices like these is a true balance, one that truly helps you rather than disguise the damage it is doing.

For what it is worth, I personally believe that seeking out this sense of balance is the most important and most effective way of benefitting from reiki.

Deep Relaxation

Relaxation is one of the most important experiences that human beings can have. We need relaxation. We constantly seek it out. Some of us use harmful techniques to relax such as taking drugs or alcohol. Some of us garden. Some of us read. Others meditate. When we relax we enter a very peaceful state. We often notice a change in our perception of time, some of us slowing down and feeling like there are more hours in the day to enjoy. Other people have the opposite experience and find that time went by quickly without them noticing but instead of feeling exhausted they feel peaceful. This is because the time was lost to something that fills their soul up with goodness.

Despite the fact that we all have things we love doing to relax, many of us simply don't do them. I know that when I take a walk at night, I will feel much better. I will have more energy to spend with my family and friends, I will sleep better and I will bring a much richer energy into my life. Yet I can't tell you how many times I have skipped my relaxing walk in order to make up lost time on different business projects. If this has happened to me as many times as it has, then it is safe to say that it has happened to you and to everyone you know. So many of us get lost inside of ourselves and forget the importance of relaxation.

One of the things that reiki brings into your life is a deep, rich and full experience of relaxation. This begins with the session itself. You get to step away from the office or home and enter into a clinic. A reiki clinic is much more relaxing than your doctor's office is. From the moment you enter, you will notice that there is a positive energy in the building. Part of this comes from the practice the building is used for but the bigger part is that many clinics are designed to be peaceful. It's like going to get a massage: as soon as you step in the door there is an energy that comes from both your optical and olfactory senses. Every reiki clinic you encounter will be set up to invite you to relax but the best ones follow the 'rules' of feng shui to maximize this effect.

This relaxation will continue as you are brought into the room where the reiki is to be performed. You will be laid down on a comfortable massage table and your reiki master will begin running their hands over your body. It is important to remember that this isn't a massage. Your reiki master is not going to be worrying about working your body in a physical manner. They are working to pass positive, healing energies from them to you. Many people find that this experience is so peaceful that they fall into a deep state of relaxation and many people even fall into a peaceful trance or a deep sleep, only to be shocked when it ends.

We spend so little time living in the moment when we relax that it can be hard to realize that was what we were trying to do. The reiki experience is designed in such a way that it makes it easy to fall into the moment, into the relaxation. This helps to relieve stress, fatigue, anxiety and even depression. This relaxation doesn't just last during the session, either. People find that the relaxation they feel during their session leaves them in a "relaxation afterglow" for days afterwards.

Remove Energy Blockages

One of the great negatives of the world is how it eats up our energy without us ever being aware. Many of us go through life with our heads down, not thinking much about anything in particular. Maybe we're worrying about the bills we have to pay or maybe we're wondering if we should ask out that cute barista at the coffee shop on the corner. Whatever it is that occupies us, it is within this that we are focused.

As we narrow our focus down on our problems and get lost in our heads, something else is happening to us. It isn't just that we are missing out on the world around us, though that is certainly true, but rather what is happening is that we are losing track of our energy expenditure. Each and every one of us is a master of multiple types of energy. There is the physical energy that we generate when we move, there is the mental energy that we use to tackle challenges and brain-twisters and then there is the spiritual energy which we carry with us. Each of these energies help to support each other.

When we have an issue with our physical energy, we often nap or sleep and wake up feeling much more able to take on physical challenges. Our mental energy is a little harder to refill, though sleeping certainly helps. Our mental energy is often spent throughout the day and this is why it is so relaxing and refreshing to sit back after work and watch a movie, listen to music or read a book. This is a way of regaining that energy.

Spiritual energy is much harder to get back. The problem with spiritual energy is, first and foremost, the simple fact that there are so many people who don't realize it exists. You can't really point to it in a biology textbook. Spiritual energy doesn't so much reside within our body the way our physical energy does. Rather, it is an energy that suffuses all of our existence; consciousness itself has been argued as being the root of spiritual energy, though I am not so sure if I personally believe this. What I do believe is that we experience a great deal of negativity due to a lack of spiritual energy.

Seeing that spiritual energy interacts with physical and mental energy, there are times when we wake up after a good night sleep but we're still too exhausted to do anything. This isn't a physical energy we're lacking but the spiritual energy necessary to compel us forward through life. Without spiritual energy, our physical and mental energy suffers. Spiritual energy is harder to heal. Some people turn to meditation. Others turn to drugs like psychedelics. Some try breathing techniques like holotropic breathwork.

One thing that we can do to really clean out those energy blockages is to undergo reiki treatment at regular intervals. Reiki treatment helps us to open up our spiritual energy and let it flow into our bodies. It's a bit like knocking the mud out of a garden hose. All of the energy was in the hose but a blockage made it hard to get at; once the negativity is removed then the hose can work again at full strength. There was never anything wrong with the hose itself, there was just a bunch of muck blocking it up. Reiki is how we clean the hose of our spiritual energy.

Clear the Mind

One of the most important practices that you can adapt today in order to improve your life is mindfulness. Mindfulness is simply the act of being in the present moment. Rather than worrying about a past that has come and gone or stressing over a future that could play out in an infinite amount of different ways, mindfulness teaches us to remember the present moment and to see it as it is. This doesn't necessarily mean that the present moment is always good, sometimes we feel awful and there is just no getting around that. Scientific studies have proven the value of mindfulness.

Mindfulness is basically at the root of a lot of Buddhist teaching. The Buddha taught that to be mindful of the present is to practice seeing it as it is and this is a powerful, important and beneficial technique which everyone should learn. This might sound as an aside to reiki but only for a minute. Reiki has its own role to play in this discussion, don't worry. I would be remiss not to mention mindfulness when discussing clearing our mind or rebalancing our energy. Mindfulness is the easiest way that we have to reestablish this balance.

Not everyone is very good at mindfulness. The techniques of mindfulness are easy to learn but people still seem to have difficulty with it. What I have seen in my own experience is that the enemy of mindfulness isn't really the techniques or the difficulty of them. Like I said, they're extremely easy. The problem with mindfulness is that many people don't realize what it is to be mindful. They think of meditation and mindfulness as a way of shutting off the brain, of quieting down all the thoughts inside of ourselves but this just isn't true. This is a false perception and it is this false perception that has caused many people to have issues with mindfulness. They are looking to achieve an effect that isn't in line with the teachings or goals of mindfulness.

When we get lost in a false perception like this, sometimes what is needed isn't more teaching but a shortcut. Reiki can serve as that shortcut. When you are first learning mindfulness, it can be hard to be mindful of anything. You're focusing on the wrong effect and you get lost in your thoughts and then feel like a failure. When you get lost, you aren't supposed to stop. You're supposed to bring your attention back to the object of your focus, most often your breath.

If you are having trouble with mindfulness then try reiki. It isn't that reiki will make you more mindful but rather it is easier to focus on the present moment within a reiki session. Focus on the way the energy is moving between the master and you: Does it feel warm? Does it feel cold? Does it leave a tingling sensation? By focusing your attention entirely on the reiki session, you can be mindful of the experience. This is a fantastic way to start practicing mindfulness as a whole, plus it is a great way to really invest yourself in the reiki experience and see how it feels to undergo it.

Breathe in and focus your attention purely on the session. This focal point will help you to be mindful of the experience. Learning to be mindful in this manner isn't just useful for reiki sessions. You can take the mindfulness lesson from your session and apply it to other areas in your life. This helps you to slow down your reactions to situations and circumstances so that you act intentionally rather than on autopilot. By being mindful, you can select the response you want rather than act on instinct.

Promote Better Sleep

While the biggest benefit of reiki treatment is the way that it lets us relax and recalibrate our spiritual energy, we shouldn't avoid the realm of the physical when discussing it. Relaxing is amazing for our souls and it helps us to feel better. This effect isn't just seen for the rest of the day after a session. This effect actually follows us into the bedroom at the end of the day as well.

When we discussed our three key forms of energy, we saw that they are physical, mental and spiritual. Our physical and our mental energy can, often, both be refreshed by sleep. Sleep doesn't always refresh them, though. Sometimes we can hit the hay early and still wake up feeling as exhausted as when we went to sleep. To understand this we must take a moment to consider how sleep works.

Those who haven't studied sleep think that it is simply a state of being. You are asleep or you are awake just like you are running or you aren't. A cursory glance would seem to confirm this idea but this isn't how sleep works. There are different levels of sleep. When you lay down and shut your eyes, you are still awake. Your consciousness is active and most of us would find that our brains are sometimes the most active when we first lay down. If you were asked, I think it would be a safe bet to claim that you are still awake at this stage. If you are thirsty in this state then you are perfectly capable of getting up and pouring yourself a drink of water. Therefore, it is easy to see this is still awake.

What about the next step? You're laying there in your bed, the warm blankets over you and you start to slip into unconsciousness. As you are laying there, in and out of unconsciousness, are you awake or are you asleep? Are you occupying both states? At this point, it becomes much harder for you to say whether or not you are asleep. If you were thirsty here, the chances that you get up for a glass of water are quite slim. As you slip deeper into your rest, you may consider yourself slipping deeper into sleep.

This, however, is an illusion. What you are slipping into at this state is the first stage of sleep. You might think you're going deeper but the truth is you aren't actually. Yes, you are going somewhere else. You can tell this because of the way that your consciousness seems to just shut off. Unless we have mastered lucid dreaming then we aren't going to be conscious of this at all and therefore we consider it to be sleep. This is simply the earliest stage of sleep. In fact, it is so early that we aren't dreaming yet. We have no way of bringing what we experience in this first stage of sleep back with us. The dreams that we associate with sleep don't begin until REM sleep starts and this takes our body quite some time to get to. Yet, it is REM sleep that is the most important for our restfulness.

When we spend the night tossing and turning, we aren't properly getting ourselves into REM sleep. Instead what is happening is that we have unwillingly trapped ourselves in the early stage of sleep. We might still be unconscious but we aren't triggering all the beneficial effects of deep sleep such as the way the body naturally releases human growth hormone when we sleep to repair our body. We aren't actually repairing or replacing any of the energy we spent the day before. We might still have our eyes closed at night but we're not sleeping correctly.

One of the tricks for getting better sleep is to practice mindfulness as we lay in bed. This can help us and since it is so easy to do I want to recommend integrating it into your daily routine. Another way that we can improve our sleep is to receive a reiki session. Reiki helps us to break up those energy blockages and to find deep relaxation and together these two elements make it much easier to fall asleep, fully and deeply. Being able to get to sleep easier at night means more time spent recovering and this results in more energy the next day and the day after.

Regular reiki sessions can help to overcome some forms of insomnia and they really do wonders by helping you to take back control of your sleeping patterns.

Improve Spiritual Growth

Spiritual growth and spiritual energy aren't the same thing. Spiritual energy is more like the gas that fills up a car's tank. It can be expended and refilled. Spiritual growth isn't quite the tank itself, though the more spiritual growth we experience then the larger our fuel tank is likely to be. This isn't a 1-for-1 metaphor, unfortunately. It is more like spiritual growth represents how the engine of that car works overall. The size of the fuel tank may be one element that increases but it isn't the only one.

As we build this metaphor out, we should be careful to consider the size of the tank a little more. It would be easy to say, "Those who have experienced more spiritual growth have more room for spiritual energy," but again this isn't always the case. You meet people all the time who are still early on the path of their spiritual growth and yet they have lots of spiritual energy. These people come with a fuel tank that is naturally bigger than other people's. This isn't to say that they are better or more spiritual compared to another; energy distribution doesn't really follow any rules or regulations.

As we move down a spiritual path, we experience spiritual growth. Activities like mindfulness and meditation can help us to take steps in this journey, to move us further along the road of the spiritual. Mindfulness and meditation are just two of the techniques we can use. There are thousands of different techniques which can fuel spiritual growth depending on your own spiritual opinions. A Buddhist will have a different view of spirituality and spiritual growth compared to a Christian. The relationship that we have with our spiritual connection differs from person to person.

One way that we can help to promote spiritual growth is through reiki. Reiki aims to help open up blockages, promote relaxation and inspire mindfulness. As a technique to promote positive health, it is first and foremost a spiritual technique. Reiki is often put forward as an answer for serious medical issues but, even as a believer, I have a hard time seeing how reiki would help against something like cancer. It isn't radiation or chemotherapy and it isn't going to kill the cancer growth. It will help the individual to better be able to withstand and deal with the negative energies that surround cancer but not the cancer itself.

Reiki is at its most powerful and effective when it is being used to tackle issues relating to the spiritual; the spiritual growth that it fosters is incredibly profound. If you are on any kind of spiritual journey whatsoever then you should try reiki. You might find that it isn't right for you but there is the very real possibility that it might be exactly what you were looking for. Either way, you won't know until you try it.

Help to Improve Mood

All of the benefits that we've looked at so far play a role in helping to improve mood: being able to relax helps to improve our mood; being able to fall asleep easily and wake feeling refreshed is certainly great when it comes to regulating our moods, being in the present, freeing up energy blockages and promoting spiritual growth are all absolutely fantastic for your mood.

These are, however, only a few of the things that are helped. We could point towards one benefit and say that helps with mood but let us instead focus our attention on the chemical process of the body itself. One of the main contributing factors to a bad mood is the presence of cortisol present within the body. Cortisol is sometimes called the stress hormone because it is directly related to stress. When you are feeling stressed, have you noticed how it seems to be more than just an emotional issue? It would be one thing if we felt stressed out and it temporarily upset our mood. When we're stressed out, though, we can feel it all throughout our bodies. This happens because there are cortisol receptors all throughout the body.

In fact, most of the cells in your body have cortisol receptors. Basically, they suck in cortisol when it is present in the body and they react to it. Cortisol helps the body out in lots of ways, as it helps to control blood sugar levels and it may even help with forming memories. Cortisol also, historically, warned us when something dangerous was present that we needed to be aware of. This was important in our evolutionary history because it could mean the difference between life and death. Cortisol levels would spike when a predator was spotted, for example, to warn us to be careful or we might end up being eaten. Cortisol plays an extremely important role in our bodies; the modern day lifestyle we live in the technologized world is one that could be thought of as cortisol-run-rampant.

We are stressed all the time, there is so much cortisol pumping through us. Marketing and technology-induced communications have greatly damaged our bodies and our moods thanks to the amount of cortisol our bodies now produce. I would never want to come across as looking down on technology. It would be impossible for me to produce this book if not for the wonders of technology. I wouldn't be able to keep in touch with friends and family as easily as I do without technology. But technology is a tool that is meant to help us progress as human beings. The tool, as we have made it currently, is broken. There's a sharp edge sticking out from it and we constantly poke ourselves with it: it doesn't cause us to bleed, it causes us to stress.

We have more cortisol in our bodies than ever before in history and we wonder why there is such a rampant wave of depression and anxiety in our current society. We have taught ourselves that we should be okay with carrying stress with us at all times. It isn't so much that we were taught this as much as we convinced ourselves of it. Look at all the memes that people share these days about being exhausted, hating their jobs or just plain being anxious and upset. These are shared as jokes but everyone sharing and liking them are saying, "Yes, I understand this feeling." We like the memes but do we ever stop and question if this is really normal?

Turns out, it really isn't. This extra stress that we carry around with us all the time weighs on us and it greatly affects our quality of life and how we feel at any given moment. Reiki is one of the tools that we can use to improve our mood by really blasting our cortisol and lowering the levels we are experiencing. When you feel the relaxation and the peace that comes from a reiki session, there is just no beating it. If you are prone to carrying around a burden of stress then I urge you to book a session today and really get a sense of how reiki feels.

Your body and your mood will thank you for it.

Chapter Summary

- There are many health benefits to practicing and partaking in reiki but it is important to understand that it is not a magical cure. It isn't going to get rid of your cancer or cure your diabetes. Reiki combined with modern medicine can greatly help.

- Modern society has a hard time finding balance in the world. We're constantly under attack by notifications and non-stop emails. This lack of balance causes a great deal of discomfort, anxiety and even depression. One of the best features of reiki is how it helps us to rediscover our balance again after we've lost it.

- Reiki is an extremely relaxing experience. Many people fall into near-unconscious states when they undergo a reiki session. This deep relaxation can do wonders for the soul such as reducing stress, lowering blood pressure and reducing the risk of heart disease.

- We have a terrible habit of collecting negative energy and carrying it around with us. This is made worse because we don't realize we are doing it. This negative energy blocks up our natural energies and this causes discomfort and pain. Reiki is a way of blasting away those blockages so we can feel like our real, true selves again.

- Another great benefit is the way that reiki helps us to clear our minds. We often have very negative thoughts and perceptions that we carry around with us. We don't realize that they are wrong because we often see them as the only way things can be. Reiki helps us to open our third eye and see reality as it is.

- Sleep is one of the most important things that we do. It helps us to heal, it recharges us and it even feels fantastic. So many people suffer from an inability to sleep. Studies on reiki and interviews with those that have undergone reiki healing show an increased ability to sleep and they report waking feeling more rested than normal.

- Every human being has a spiritual self, even if they haven't thought much about it. Practicing reiki or getting reiki treatments is a great way to start getting in touch with your spiritual side and this promotes a deeper investigation of the spiritual and leads to much growth.

- Reiki is enjoyable. It just plain feels good. It is relaxing, it clears out negativity and it promotes good health. Is it any surprise that people report feeling much happier after undergoing reiki treatment?

In the next chapter you will learn about the five most important kinds of reiki. These range from Usui reiki, named after the founder, through to the Egyptian seichim reiki. While the majority of this book focuses on Usui reiki, these others are important to learn about.

CHAPTER THREE

TYPES OF REIKI

Talking about reiki in the West, we are most often talking about Usui reiki. If we speak about reiki in the East, we are most often talking about jikiden reiki. These are the two biggest types of reiki being practiced in the world today but they aren't the only methods.

We aren't going to talk about every type of reiki being practiced today. One practice that we'll be avoiding is rainbow reiki. This form is based closely on Usui reiki but it brings astral travel and healing crystals into the reiki session. Rainbow reiki also claims that angels and gods are involved in the healing process itself, which pushes it into a realm closer to religion than the purely spiritual. Another type of reiki that we won't be spending our time on is kundalini reiki, which was developed by a Danish master. This type of reiki focuses on personal development and focuses more on overcoming issues like impotence or a lack of grounding. Kundalini reiki drops a lot of the elements you see in traditional reiki and instead uses philosophies derived from earth and sky energies. As such, both of these practices are more unique and specific forms of reiki that move away from the roots of the practice.

It is these roots that we are focusing on in this volume and so it should come as no surprise that we will be starting our look at the various types of reiki connected with Usui reiki. From there we will move into jikiden reiki, karuna, lightarian and seichim reiki practices. These five practices will show us the similarities and differences between the various reiki practices; we're going to focus our attention on the benefits that each type offers, as it is these benefits that are the most interesting component.

When you are preparing to book your first reiki appointment, you will want to ask which type of reiki your provider is practicing. They should be able to answer your question without any problems. If there are problems, then I don't recommend that you work with that practitioner. Conversely, just because someone can answer quickly doesn't mean they're a good fit, either. Learning the benefits from each of these reiki practices will help you decide which type is best for you. Whenever possible, stick with that type of reiki that resonates with you when booking appointments.

REIKI HEALING

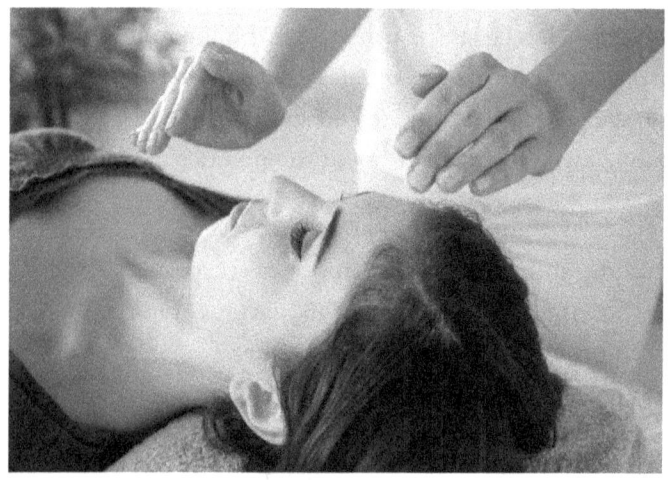

Usui Reiki

Even though it is often thought of as Western reiki, Usui reiki makes up the largest chunk of any of the reiki practices with nearly a whopping 90% of all reiki practitioners using a form of Usui reiki. Considering that it sources back to the birth of reiki, this is a solid choice.

Usui reiki is taught according to four aspects. These are healing practice, personal development, spiritual discipline and mystic order. Together, these four aspects are combined with the nine elements: oral tradition, spiritual lineage, history, initiation, symbols, treatment, form of teaching, monetary exchange and precepts.

These four aspects each play with one (or more) of the nine elements to make up the Usui approach. If this is confusing now, don't worry, it will remain this way. This is one of the harder aspects of reiki to understand and it often feels as if each practitioner has their own understanding of how the aspects and elements come together. Rather than focus on this aspect, which masters are still known to grapple with, let us turn our attention to the benefits of Usui reiki.

The biggest benefit of Usui reiki is the fact that it is the most widely known and used. This means it is accessible to the highest number of people compared to the other styles. If you are going to get a reiki treatment done then the chances are good that what you are receiving is a treatment using Usui reiki. Even if you've never heard of reiki before and signed up for a session off the street, it is most likely Usui reiki.

Usui reiki is a non-invasive healing technique. This means that there is minimal to no pain. In fact, some people swear that reiki has even helped to diminish their pain. This is a questionable area to discuss; with cancer and serious medical issues, it is always best to combine a practice like reiki with the knowledge of modern medicine. Much of the pain that we experience falls into the following two categories. The first category is pain which we have created ourselves; the pain we feel comes from the way that we have hijacked our own brains and created a phantom pain. Another category is made up of pains that aren't so bad on their own but we have blown them out of proportion. One of the benefits of reiki is that pain that primarily establishes itself at the mental and the spiritual levels can be blown apart and destroyed by reiki, making your life a much less painful experience subjectively.

Reiki can help you to reduce stress, reestablish balance and open yourself up to deep relaxation. All of these are benefits that Usui reiki clearly promotes and enjoys. Along with these benefits is a focus on accepting ourselves as we are. One of the places that pain and discomfort comes from is the false perceptions we have of ourselves. Reiki helps to clean these away and many people find that they can connect with themselves in a deep and meaningful way after a reiki session. One of the reasons for this is the way that hidden emotions and feelings often come out in a reiki session. Remember our hose metaphor from the last chapter? If we are blocked up, then we need to clear that blockage. Sometimes what we find when we clear out our blockages is that there was something hidden behind it. It's like when we distract ourselves with TV. We ignore our problems by watching the TV but then when the power goes out we have nothing left to do but confront ourselves. Only reiki is more enjoyable than TV and it is more like the lights going on rather than them flickering off.

As a practice, reiki is safe for pretty much everyone. The moments when reiki becomes problematic is when it is offered as the solution to problems it isn't equipped to deal with. Rather than viewing reiki as an off/on or yes/no or either/or dichotomy with modern medicine, remember to see them as friends. Reiki can help to keep your spiritual and emotional self feeling great, seeing with an open perspective and relaxing to improve your sleep and minimize stress and anxiety. To practice reiki at the detriment of your medical care is a bad idea and one that can cause a lot of damage.

That said, Usui reiki is recommended for small and non-life threatening injuries. These injuries can't be treated with modern medicine beyond putting on a bandaid, maybe a little disinfectant and taking a painkiller. Often it is these little injuries that lead to issue with opiate abuse and chronic pain syndromes. Rather than reaching for a chemical painkiller, try booking a reiki session and seeing if you experience pain relief. This can be a way of increasing your own ability to deal with life's pains. It isn't so much that reiki makes the pain go away, though this can certainly be an effect, but what is more important is that reiki helps us to reprogram and change the way that we react to and experience pain. If we can reduce the discomfort that pain brings into our lives then we immediately reduce much of the negativity of pain.

These, along with all the reasons we discussed in the previous chapter, are among the benefits of Usui reiki. I would like to recommend Usui reiki over the other forms, though this speaks to my own natural bias.

Jikiden Reiki

Jikiden reiki is most often practiced in the East. Translated into English, jikiden would be "to hand down without changing or translating." That is to say, the reiki practices within this practice were handed down directly from practitioner to practitioner, tracing back to Usui himself much more directly than any of the other modern-day practices of Usui reiki. It is a little complicated, since Usui is the root of both Usui and jikiden reiki; the one named after him is actually the least straightforward of the two.

Consider it like a martial art. There is this great teacher, let's say he trained someone like Bruce Lee. He starts a dojo and he trains five instructors under him. From there, four of those instructors head out into the world and they learn their own lessons and add those to what they teach their students. But one of those instructors stayed behind and stuck as close to the first teacher's lessons as they could. As those other martial artists have slight variations or sometimes incredibly large differences between what they originally learned and what they taught, there remains one path that stays as close as possible to the original. Jikiden reiki is the closest that modern reiki comes to the original.

Jikiden reiki has the most traditional approach to reiki out of those we're looking at. This is beneficial because it makes it a very pure version of the practice, as close to the original discovery of it as possible. It continues to be a non-invasive form of healing. It is a great practice for helping to recover from injuries in concert with modern medicine. For example, it will help your leg to heal but if you don't set the bone when it breaks then all the healing in the world isn't going to matter.

Jikiden reiki has a strong focus on removing negative and harmful habits and mental processes from the brain. Its goals are tied closely to its Buddhist origin but this in no way means that this is a faith-based healing approach. You don't need to be a Buddhist to benefit from jikiden reiki. Christians and atheists both can enjoy the positive effects associated with jikiden reiki. The focus is on habits and ways that we create our own suffering and so there is nothing like praising God or healing our soul. Everyone has spiritual energy but this isn't the same as religious energy. Increasing our spiritual energy can help us to see ourselves clearly to remove those negative qualities. Jikiden reiki helps us with this.

REIKI HEALING

One benefit that jikiden reiki has in regards to life improvement is the way it helps us to overcome substances and other addictions. Jikiden reiki helps us to see ourselves clearly and see what activities are bringing a negative energy into our lives and this helps us to get control over them. Jikiden reiki sessions can be used as a way to check-in with yourself and see the progress you've made since your last session, all while gathering the energy necessary to change for the better while you're waiting for your next appointment.

Karuna Reiki

Karuna reiki comes from the Sanskrit word karuna which means to act compassionately to reduce others' suffering. This term is used in both Buddhism and Hinduism. It is very hard to capture the deepest meaning of this compassionate action as it comes from enlightenment and, while you can use words to describe enlightenment, one of the concepts behind enlightenment is its inability to be described. Enlightenment is something that is felt. With enlightenment there is a deep sense of how everyone is connected and how pain in one functions to hurt the whole of mankind.

Some say that karuna reiki is among the strongest forms of reiki, though I don't personally share this view. The idea here is that this form of reiki is achieved through channeling the healing energy of love through the hands. It is considered to be a more advanced version of reiki and there are some practitioners who are quite powerful by all accounts. As a more advanced version of reiki, there are higher prices that can be asked for with it and this makes it a prime way for con artists to swindle money from the public. If you are looking to experience karuna reiki then you absolutely must look into and research the practitioner you are considering making an appointment with. This is extremely important. Find out what other people are saying and if they've ever had any major complaints against them. Small things are typically fine to ignore but big complaints and problems will be obvious quite quickly. This will help you to avoid getting taken advantage of.

You might think that because of the ease of getting taken advantage of that people might be best avoiding karuna reiki. While I think that usui and jikiden are better approaches, especially for those that haven't experienced reiki before, there are lots of benefits said to come from karuna reiki and they are pretty attractive. As you'll see from the following list, there are valid reasons why someone might want to seek out this form of reiki.

Karuna reiki is as non-invasive as the rest, a theme of reiki in general and one of the reasons it is so attractive to people. Most forms of reiki, however, are meant to be done on people who are awake and aware of the process. Karuna reiki on the other hand is said to work on those who are unconscious. At first this might seem a little odd. Why would someone want reiki if they aren't even awake? Consider a patient in a coma: while the doctors keep them healthy physically, karuna reiki can be added to the mixture to help heal them spiritually, too. Many people believe that a healthy spirit is an important part of coming out of a coma. Again, however, I am of the mind that spiritual healing of this nature, even if it can have a physical effect, is best combined with modern medical practices. It is the fusion of these two worlds that will see us evolve as a species.

Because karuna reiki has such a strong focus on the love felt for the other person it can be quite good for helping those that suffer from panic attacks or other anxiety disorders. A lot of the time these problems can seem utterly devastating. Not just because of the way they make a person feel but because of the way friends and family react to anxiety and depression. This can often leave a person feeling helpless and a bother to other people; this leads many suffering from these mental illnesses to think that the people around them think poorly of them. Karuna reiki focuses on love and compassion and this direction makes it clear that the practitioner cares about a person's pain and their mental wellbeing, even when they are feeling low. This can make reiki very therapeutic in a mental way, though it can be dangerous when a practitioner doesn't know very much about depression. The best reiki practitioners for those suffering from mental health issues are karuna reiki practitioners with an education in psychology and psychiatry.

Karuna reiki can be quite invigorating and this has a positive effect in reducing and minimizing pain and fatigue. Less pain and less fatigue is one of the reasons why karuna reiki is so good at helping people to get their sleep schedule back on track: it makes it easier for the body to hear and listen to the natural circadian rhythms we each experience. Being able to sleep is great because this in turn helps to reduce the pain in the body, increase the amount of energy a person experiences throughout the day and has been shown in studies to be strongly linked to a person's sense of wellbeing and happiness.

When we are more happy, we are better at taking care of ourselves and we are better at planning for our futures. All of us need to slow down and stay in the moment more, which reiki helps with; when we get too sad or too lost in the struggles of life, we often stop taking care of ourselves properly or planning for our futures. Karuna reiki helps people to visualize and manifest their dreams and desires. It isn't some magic that you simply wish for. Rather, it helps you to see the way you must live in order to achieve your goals. The negative patterns we fall into have to change for us to achieve our goals and reiki is good for this, especially karuna reiki. As we work on changing ourselves, we reduce the amount of influence that negative energies have in our lives, over our minds and over our bodies.

Many people report that karuna reiki helps them to get over pain. This pain can be physical but many people strongly express that the physical pain relief pales in comparison to the emotional pain they have been able to overcome. It isn't rare to find stories where people say they spent entire sessions crying. At the end of the session, they emphasize the fact that it made them feel so much better. Honestly, a lot of us don't cry enough. Especially men. Being able to identify emotional pain and sort it out with someone who is there to support you and help you through it is a powerful, powerful experience that is beneficial to everyone. This kind of emotional healing can help you on the path of overcoming childhood trauma and deep-rooted issues.

Issues such as relationship abuse, codependency, addiction, depression, denial, poor communication, all of these and more are the concern of karuna reiki. Because it approaches from the direction of pure compassion and love it is much more open to helping those deep problems which hurt so many people. It really can help to clear the mind, mend the body and heal the soul.

I need to again emphasize how important it is to be mindful and careful of who you select to work with when it comes to karuna reiki. Issues as deeply rooted and as serious as these should never be taken lightly. Always research the person you are considering and speak with them prior to booking. Ask how they came to be trained in reiki and if they have any other formal education. Find out their philosophy when it comes to reiki and how they practice it. You don't want to give money to a con artist who could exacerbate your mental, physical and spiritual ills any more than they already are.

Only give your money to certified, professional and honest practitioners of karuna reiki, those who have earned the right to call themselves masters of this form of healing.

Lightarian Reiki

This form of reiki is considered to be another step along the line of Usui and karuna reiki. It is considered to be a higher form of reiki and as such it is only practiced by masters who have put in the time and experience to practice their skills. It is also only practiced by those who have been able to attend to and stick with a spiritual path. It requires a lot of spiritual practice and experience in order to become a master of lightarian reiki.

When people describe reiki, they often talk of the vibrational bands upon which it is founded. It is said that these bands and the way that they vibrate are how reiki practitioners tap into their healing energies. This vibration energy gives us the effect. Following this theory, there are eight bands. Usui reiki makes up the first band, karuna reiki makes up the second. Lightarian reiki practitioners maintain that the third through to the eighth vibrational bands are used by lightarian reiki. Each of these bands is representative of a different level of attunement. The idea is that lightarian reiki provides much more healing ability than any of the others; each band that a master attunes to gives them more healing power.

This type of reiki uses all of the same symbols from Usui reiki, as it was the intention to keep reiki as simple as possible. Those that practice lightarian reiki are said to first heal themselves through the process of opening up to the energy of each additional band. The practitioner is thus able to use the healing powers of lightarian reiki both for themselves and for others.

Lightarian reiki doesn't necessarily have any benefits that haven't already been discussed during our look at Usui or karuna reiki. It isn't that opening up to the additional vibrational bands equals more healing ability. You can't use a hammer to cut wood, you have to first select the proper tool to cut the wood. Likewise, you can't suddenly levitate people or heal cancer simply by opening up further vibrational levels. What you do achieve is a healing effect that is faster and more effective. It makes it easier and more achievable to heal with reiki like you would with the others. What might take a lot of work with Usui practice can be achieved more easily and quickly using lightarian reiki.

Seichim Reiki

This type of reiki is sometimes called sekehem reki. While the others primarily come from or tie their roots back to Japan, seichim reiki comes from Egypt. It is said to have originally come from the Egpytian goddess Sekhmet. If we tie reiki back to Usui then seichim or sekehem isn't technically reiki at all. If we do tie reiki to palm healing based on vibrational frequencies then, yes, this would be. Seichim reiki is a form of gentle and loving healing as it comes from a goddess, but a tough goddess, so it is said to have the strength to rip through barriers and emotional or energy blockages.

This form of reiki is closely connected to the elements of air, earth, fire, spirit and water. These are said to be the natural elements which make up this process. While many people think the four elements are air, earth, fire and water, those who walk this spiritual path believe that spirit is a big component of the elements and it is part of the other four elements. If the four elements were mixed up together in a cocktail then spirit would be the glass that holds them: you couldn't have the four elements without spirit. These elements are combined with an understanding of chakras and seichim reiki even makes use of a mixture of ancient symbols and quantum mechanics. It makes for a very complex healing system, not at all like the simplicity demonstrated by lightarian reiki.

A treatment with seichim reiki is quite a bit different compared to other reiki treatments. Most forms of reiki produce a palpable feeling as the master works the energy in the room through their body and into yours. This feeling tends to be sustained, often quite minor. It might have peaks and valleys depending on where it is being performed on your body at any given moment but these are rather minor when compared to seichim reiki. Seichim reiki is reported to build and build in intensity as a session continues. The longer the session, the more intense the process feels. It has a much deeper, harder energy to control than the other forms we've looked at. The essential oils used in the process of seichim reiki can help to make the experience more enjoyable and the effects are supposed to last for upwards of a week afterwards.

A key to seichim reiki is the way that it focuses on improving and breaking free blockages in your life and its key focus is getting rid of the negativity that weighs us down. It can be hard to really achieve anything when we're bogged down with an abundance of bad energy. Right now, you might be having a good day: you woke up early and were able to get the kids to school on time, prepared lunch, squeezed in some cleaning and even caught up on some sports coverage you missed. That's a pretty great day. You might say that was you at full energy. But negative energy might be weighing you down without you even realizing it. You might be tapping into only 60% of your total energy and thinking it was full because 40% is constantly being wasted by negative energy. Seichim reiki aims to get rid of negative energy.

The negative energy that seichim reiki deals with is wide-ranging. Some people simply have stressful lives and have to deal with the negative energy that comes from their day-to-day lifestyle. Other people may be dealing with the loss of a loved one or they might be losing their job or dealing with kids that have gotten into drugs recently. Any number of life events can generate a whole whack of negative energy and there isn't a whole lot that can be done about it because most of us don't realize we're carrying it with us. Seichim reiki is one way of getting rid of the negative energies in your life, regardless of whether the source is small things or big things.

Other benefits associated with seichim reiki include the speed at which people heal. Those that have undergone seichim reiki report that they feel themselves healing much faster than with the other forms. It is also said that seichim reiki is better at opening people up to the spiritual pathways of this life. Along with healing comes a sense of completeness and a confidence in our abilities that helps us to bring our goals to life. When negative energy is cleared away, it is much easier to see the world around us clearly, as well as ourselves. This clarity can cause us to feel more alive than we've ever felt before and it is amazing. It is as if the present moment opened itself up and showed how much happiness and wealth of experience there is around us at any moment.

Seichim reiki is a very powerful form of reiki, though it is quite hard to find. You really need to seek this one out if you want it and it just might be worth it.

Chapter Summary

- There are many types of reiki, though we focus our attention on the five big ones.

- Less widely practiced forms of reiki include rainbow reiki, which claims to get its power from angels and gods, and kundalini reiki, which focuses on overcoming personal issues.

- Usui reiki is the most widely taught form, with 90% of all reiki being taught today being Usui. This is why we primarily focus on Usui reiki in this book.

- Usui reiki is sometimes referred to as Western reiki the same way that the second degree of reiki often is.

- Usui reiki is taught with the four aspects of healing practice, personal development, spiritual discipline and mystic order; which combine with the nine elements: oral tradition, spiritual lineage, history, initiation, symbols, treatment, form of teaching, monetary exchange and precepts.

- Usui reiki is easily accessible to anyone that is interested in learning it.

- Jikiden reiki is more commonly practiced in the East than in the West. It translates to "handed down without changing." This name comes from the fact that jikiden reiki is as close to the original form as possible, with each master handing down the teachings without changing or altering them.

- Jikiden reiki is a more traditional form of reiki and it has a strong focus on removing negative and harmful habits or mental processes, which directly links it to its Buddhist origins.

- Karuna reiki is a form of reiki which focuses on reducing the pain of others for compassionate reasons. It focuses on healing others from a purely compassionate point of view.

- Karuna reiki is said to be the most powerful form of reiki but it is also one that is often claimed by con artists to trick unsuspecting people into giving away their money.

- When karuna reiki is performed by a master, you can tell. There is such an energy that can be felt.

- Lightarian reiki is considered a step up from Usui and karuna reiki. Usui reiki is said to tap into the first band of vibrational energy while karuna reiki taps into the second. There are six more bands of vibration energy and lightarian reiki uses all of them.

- Lightarian reiki uses the same symbols as Usui reiki in order to keep it simple.

- Seichim reiki is a form of reiki from Egypt. From all appearances it seems to not actually be a form of reiki but to be a similar practice which gets lumped together with the others. It is connected to the elements of air, earth, fire, spirit and water rather than the elements that Usui reiki is connected to.

- Seichim reiki is said to build and build throughout a session and it has a much stronger and hotter energy than the other forms of reiki do.

In the next chapter you will see what a typical reiki session looks like. We start with booking our very first appointment and discuss how to pick a practitioner who will treat you professionally. From there you will learn how long a typical session will take, what happens during a session, what you feel while the session is going on, what you can do during the session to make it more enjoyable and what you can do after to keep the experience positive.

CHAPTER FOUR

A TYPICAL REIKI SESSION

Reiki sessions can be extremely varied. There isn't any official guideline as to how a session should be handled. This can lead to a lot of differences between various practitioners in different countries, states or even towns who may have completely different approaches than their neighbors.

Reiki can be practiced anywhere at any time. If you are too sick to leave a hospital bed then a practitioner can come to your hospital. Likewise if you are confined to your home. This creates too much variation to call any of these sessions typical in terms of the setting. For this chapter to work we are going to imagine going to a practitioner that takes patients in at their own location. This is the way that most people will first experience reiki, so it is perfect for beginners. Do know that there are all sorts of different reiki classes and sessions with different settings such as doing reiki in the park or a reiki-camping getaway. You can find out about opportunities like these through your local practitioners but we'll consider these to be atypical encounters.

We'll start by looking at the typical setting for a reiki appointment. From booking an appointment to the setting of the appointment will kick the chapter off. From there, we'll look at the duration of a session and see how it varies. We'll discuss what happens in the session, as in what you would see if you were to watch the session being done. We'll also explore the feelings that might be experienced during the session and what you should do during the session. This will get you ready to book your own and the following chapter will explore the techniques and hand positions of reiki so stick around!

The Typical Reiki Setting

Most reiki practitioners will have a space which you come to for your sessions. What this space looks like on the outside may greatly affect your experience of it. After all, an office setup inside of the city looks different than one in the surrounding countryside. Depending on the place you go for your session there could be a number of different protocols that you have to follow. Some practitioners will take walk-ins but most places will want to schedule you for an initial appointment prior to a session.

Start by first calling up your local practitioner and asking about their hours and their intake process. Find the time that works best for you and book your initial appointment. This shouldn't be any harder than doing a quick internet search for "reiki near me." Remember, once again, that you should always do a quick search online about each of the practitioners you consider. Always ensure that you are seeing a professional. While you may be tempted to ask questions on the phone based on the information on their website, try not to go into anything too complex. Confirm the kind of reiki that they practice, maybe ask about how the practitioner learned it or how the practice came to open. You should be able to gather a little bit of information about the practitioner this way but the really important moment comes with the initial interview.

While a reiki practitioner is going to want to interview you, you should also consider the first meeting as your time to interview them, too. For the practitioner, this interview is about finding out your specific needs, as well as your basic healthcare information that they should know about. There may even be a consent form involved. In fact, a consent form can be a good thing. It tells you that they do not want to get sued from people thinking that a reiki session is going to fix a major issue they have when it doesn't work that way. However, if they get you to sign a consent form but continue to act as if reiki can cure every ailment then you should not trust the practitioner.

A good practitioner will be willing to answer any of your questions and they will probably be impressed by your knowledge on the subject. The practitioner should walk you through the process even better than this chapter does. By walking you through it, they will be able to discuss any problems you might have such as conditions that limit your range of motion or how long you can stay in one position. If you have areas which can't be touched due to pain or other medical conditions then this is extremely important to share with your practitioner. While a hospital requires a reiki practitioner to get your verbal consent before they touch you, a private practice does not. It should and legally it does but this isn't a guarantee that your consent will be honored. This is important to know if you have issues about being touched. That said, a respectful practitioner won't touch you until they are given permission. This is a practice founded on compassion, after all.

When you first get to your reiki appointment, you may have to wait. This is often a place that looks like a dentist or doctor's office a lot of the time or maybe a hair salon. That means chairs, magazines, maybe one TV mounted on the wall and whatever interior design they've settled on. Most of the colors you see will be very calming. Often vibrant but never threatening. Earth tones are a favorite. Sometimes you will see blue used for its calming effect. No matter how many places you visit, they all tend to stick with a theme that promotes a sense of relaxation and peace. It would be counterintuitive to create an atmosphere that was chaotic or intense. This waiting space is often where the administrative assistant will have a desk and book appointments and it never fails that these places employ the nicest employees.

When it is time to come in, you'll be led into the space where the session will take place. This could be a room, or even a backyard, or really anything at all, it depends on the space they have available. It will have a calm atmosphere and it will often smell quite nice. Smells can be an issue for some people, however, so make sure that you mention any issues you may have with them. Gentle music is often played and different ambient effects can be achieved with the lighting. This space is one that is used for energy and with body work and so it will be kept at a reasonable temperature. You will be asked to sit or lay down, depending on what you are comfortable with, and your reiki session will begin.

Again, it can't be emphasized enough how open this is to variation. There isn't a dress code for the setting of a typical reiki session. Consider it like this: you could get a massage anywhere. You could lay down on the beach and your partner could give you a massage. If you could do it anywhere then what does a typical session look like? There isn't one. We still book appointments at massage clinics. So we use massage therapy as the example for a typical session. This is the exact same with reiki.

How Long Does a Reiki Session Last?

This is another hard-to-answer question. In fact, the questions that come after will be much easier compared to these first two. The answers to, "What is a typical reiki setting?" and, "How long does a session last?" depend on what you are looking to get out of the reiki session, where it is and who the practitioner is you are meeting with. Some practitioners have a high demand for their services and they can only meet with people for short periods of time. Yet others with high demand get that demand because they meet with people for a long time each session.

Some variation between practitioners makes a lot of sense. Surely you've met a doctor that always seemed to take forever to finish a simple procedure while other doctors were quick at it. Sometimes, too, it depends on the clients that the practitioner is meeting before you. Sometimes they take a long time and it changes the planned session. Things like this are impossible to escape in the real world. It should also be noted that special classes, trips and sessions can be scheduled to take place over the course of days.

Instead of worrying about these individual instances, let's consider an average. Once again this will be from the place where you book an appointment. In this scenario, we aren't going to consider the initial appointment interview; that's a special circumstance. The first thing that is going to affect the time it takes for your session is what you are looking to get out of it. If you have a lot of troubles and pain then you will likely need a longer session. Some practitioners like to start people slow and move up to longer sessions, others have no problem starting with lengthy sessions.

Most places report that a typical session of reiki healing lasts anywhere between twenty to ninety minutes. Again, this will differ greatly due to the different needs a person has with their reiki session. When there is a lot of healing to be done, it takes a long time to do it. Both twenty minute and ninety minute sessions are basically outliers. They are representative of the far ends of the appointment-length spectrum; the average is somewhere in the middle.

Most reiki practitioners who are intaking patients from the general population through appointment are going to have a set amount of time that they book for each session. It is far more common to find the timeframe to be around forty-five minutes. Some like sticking with half an hour but forty-five minutes allows for a thirty minute session, a little bit of room on either end for set-up and any necessary discussion and then fifteen minutes remaining to prepare the space for a new session before the next client comes.

Much like with a doctor, people like to schedule their next reiki sessions as they leave their just-completed session. These are most often check-in sessions. Check-in sessions may be on the short end, as those who are living well don't need nearly as much health managing their spiritual energy. You don't go to a doctor only when it is time to check in with them. Most of us call up and book an appointment with our doctor if we encounter some kind of emergency or complication. Reiki is the same way.

Check-in sessions are short whereas longer sessions to help deal with emotional, physical or spiritual pain are typically available with many practitioners. Practitioners of this practice care about the people they are helping and many will go out of their way to ensure that one of their clients is healthy and happy. Don't be afraid to discuss emergency sessions with your practitioner and feel free to see if they host longer sessions.

There are many people who find great relief in reiki and one of the things that is neat about the practice is the way that it is said to heal the practitioner themselves. This has led a lot of people into considering practicing reiki and it isn't hard to find workshops that teach the basics. The practitioner you see likely has taught classes from time to time. If you find that you need reiki on a more regular basis then it may be worth considering learning the skill from a master. This will allow you to have smaller sessions each day without having to book any more appointments. Typically, you can expect a session to take about an hour.

What Happens During a Reiki Session?

Let's go ahead and skip the waiting. As much as the waiting room seems to be an integral part of just about any appointment, we don't really need to go over it a second time. So let's start our session from the moment you enter the room.

Typically, the reiki session room has a massage table. This makes it extremely easy for the practitioner to perform all of the traditional healing positions of the hands. Some people can't deal with sitting down for the length of time necessary for reiki and these sessions may involve a chair or even standing. It's hard to say what the work-around that a particular reiki practitioner uses is going to be but everyone has one. It is very common for reiki practitioners to perform their services on those with medical issues and that causes a need for the reiki practitioner to be flexible.

Most places will have a massage table. Massage requires removing your clothing but that isn't a thing with reiki. Reiki is a non-invasive maneuver in more ways than one. Despite massage being a non-invasive procedure, the techniques that the massage therapist uses to work your muscles are far more invasive than reiki. In reiki, you are expected to remain completely clothed. Though I would recommend avoiding any clothing that is overly restrictive. If your clothing makes you feel trapped then it is no good. Flowing or loose fitting clothing will make the experience more comfortable.

This isn't because the experience is overly difficult. In fact, all you have to do is lay there. We'll discuss the things you need to do prior and during a session but the main thing is lay there peacefully. The reiki practitioner will move their hands over your body using touches far lighter than most massage therapists use. The point of the connection here isn't to use the physical touch to help. Rather it is about the energy passing through the palms of the practitioner which is important. The practitioner will have a set of locations over which they make sure to position their hands. This is most often around the head and the upper torso.

One fear with reiki is a fear that is common with massage: the worry about being inappropriately touched. If you have ever spoken with a massage therapist then you know the biggest issue with inappropriate touching comes from the clients and not the therapist. This is similar in reiki. Reiki is purposefully a non-intrusive procedure and your practitioner should never touch you inappropriately. There may be times in which a practitioner needs to work on your arms or legs but these are typically more rare. A massage therapist works on the body itself but a reiki practitioner is working with the chakras of the body and the parts of the body that hold onto the most negative and harmful energies. Limbs get worked out mostly when there is a problem or injury with them, for the most part reiki focuses on the upper half of a person.

As you lay there, the reiki practitioner will hold their hands in various ways which help to cover the most area while letting the energy pass through smoothly. Some practitioners don't actually touch your body but instead hover their hands above your body ever so slightly. It is best to stay still while this is happening and let the practitioner work their talent.

Most places will have some music that will help to make the atmosphere a little more ambient. Some places prefer to play the sounds of nature, which is my personal preference. There is something fitting about the sounds of the natural world that helps us to connect back deeper into ourselves and the root of what it is to be a human. We'll talk more about the music of the session in a little bit. First, let's move from what happens to how it feels while it happens.

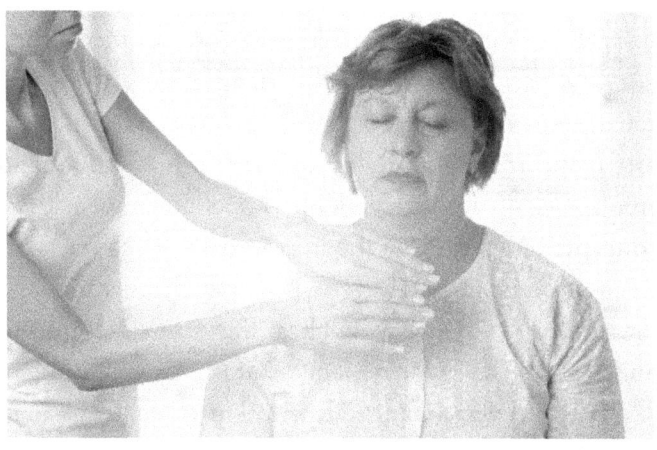

What Do You Experience During a Typical Reiki Session?

The feelings around energy are very hard to explain. Not because they are overly weird or complex. In fact, it is often quite the opposite: many people are completely shocked by how subtle and smooth the energy from a reiki session can feel. The problem with energy is that it isn't a uniform process the same way that something like heat is. If you sit down on a heater then you are going to feel hot. If you go in for a massage then your muscles will be worked through a physical process and you can describe that easily. Even those getting a massage, however, will use terminology like, "It felt like heaven," or, "It was so peaceful," which are subjective and can mean different things to different people.

This is incredibly interesting to note prior to turning our attention over to reiki. Massage is a purely physical activity and yet the language we use to describe it is quite often one that is more in line with the spiritual and emotional. What this highlights is how much we use the concepts of energy and the immaterial to describe what we are experiencing. If everyone experienced a massage the same way then we would hear the same descriptions, but everyone has an experience that is personal to them. Reiki is this way but the description often lands it in trouble. To say that everyone experiences massage differently seems fine because we can see the process of a massage in action. Since reiki healing is done through energy, it is something that must be felt and each person interprets the feelings of energy differently.

The fact that energy is different for each person is something that is universally understood by those with experience in the realm of the spiritual. There are even highly respected scientists who spend their careers researching how our perceptions of reality differ from one another. It is a captivating and fascinating field of study and one that offers great value to those spiritual few who enjoy keeping up with the sciences. Until someone understands how energy manifests and how you can detect it, it is hard to tell that anything is happening.

It isn't all that uncommon for people to be disappointed by their first reiki session. "Sure, I felt good but it didn't really feel like much of anything," isn't such a rare response. Yet many people find that their spirits, their experience of life after having a session improves. Some people find this to happen in a large way while others find it much more subtle. The realm of energy and spiritual healing is very hard to understand or rather perhaps not understand but interpret. Many of the things which arise from spiritual healing could be attributed to other causes. For example, you might be happier after your reiki session but someone else could point out many reasons a person may be happier. Or maybe someone with anger issues finds that reiki helps them to calm down but another person might just dismiss this as the way everyone seems to calm down as they age. As we train our spiritual senses through meditation and other practices we gain greater ability to spot the way that our spiritual energy opens us up to positive experience. Reiki helps with this opening and you may have to take some time to learn how to identify it.

Let's leave behind the theory and talk about actual experiences during a session. What do you feel? What is typical? Typical here is based on those experiences most commonly reported by people who have experienced reiki healing first-hand. The most common responses immediately after a session are people reporting a feeling of being refreshed, of having their energy restored to them. Another common response to reiki healing is a feeling of being more balanced, a sense that you are more present within your own body. Some people find that they pass out during the session, though not fully. This will be important in a moment. The sense of peace that comes with a session is very common in most reports. There are other reports from people who say they didn't feel anything and they were just annoyed with the experience but these aren't overly common. Some could be attributed to energy too subtle to feel, others could have experienced con artists pretending to give real reiki healing and some simply brought too much anger with them to the experience and spoiled it for themselves. With any form of spiritual healing, you can expect a certain level of negative reviews that seem to exist merely to insult the practice as a whole.

Alright, remember that sleep state we mentioned earlier? We discussed how it isn't actually so much a sleep state. People often report feeling as if they could have fallen asleep or even thinking that they did. A common experience that has been shown as of late is that many people seem to enter into a meditative state during reiki. This isn't to say that they are meditating. Well, they are but not that they are purposefully trying to. The energies working on them put them in a relaxed state of mind and this opens up their consciousness to sink down deeper into another level. They aren't fully conscious but neither are they asleep. The brain is somewhere, doing something. While it is hard to explain where the brain is, we can say that it appears to be the same place it goes during meditation proper. This is a very positive thing to note about reiki. Meditation is one of the best things you can do for your body and mind but many people feel like they are unable to do so. If you are one of these people then consider booking a reiki appointment. You'll be able to see for yourself why meditation can be so helpful. It's like being able to practice reiki-lite anywhere and anytime you want.

As for the physical feelings that people experience, they differ. As mentioned before, some people don't feel much of anything. They relax deeply, often enter a meditative state and while there they aren't aware of their body or their energies very much. Others are too body-focused and have a hard time giving into the feeling of the energy itself. This is a common experience, actually, for people both new to reiki and those new to other consciousness changing practices such as certain medicinal substances or breathing techniques used in spiritual practice. Being too focused on the body can make us uncomfortable as we over-focus our attention. Imagine you are trying to float down the river of reiki, present in the moment but there is a tree fallen over the river and you are stuck on it. This is what happens when we body-focus too strongly. We stop going with the flow and try to cling onto a particular feeling.

Those who do feel the energy from reiki report experiences with quite a range of feelings. Some find that they can feel a cold energy from where the reiki practitioners hands are located. Others claim that the energy they feel is warm. Some feel that the experience has just a slight tickle to it. Others describe sensations of waves pulsing from the practitioner's hands and entering into their body. All sorts of random sensations of a similar nature are also reported. Each person has a unique relationship to how spiritual energy feels and this can make it hard to predict how exactly it affects people in a general description.

Another issue that comes up is the fact that reiki is cumulative. Many people find that rather than having an occasional reiki session, they need a reiki routine. The cumulative nature of reiki means that people have a much easier time feeling it when they need to take more. A friend of mine has a child who is diagnosed with ADHD and they were given medication for it that was supposed to work cumulatively. For the first month, there was no change. About halfway through the second month a change occurred and they were finding the child to be much easier to control. The levels of the medication in the body had built up to a point that they were having an effect. Reiki works in this same manner, the second session builds upon the first and the third will continue to build on from the second. The feelings that arise during a session are prone to grow and evolve with the more sessions you have.

For those of you who are first starting out with reiki and experiencing it for the first time, try to look at it with open eyes. Don't go in expecting to feel all sorts of invisible forces working through you. Hey, you might. I don't want to tell you that you won't but the chances are that you won't. The chances favor a much more subtle experience. To improve how you feel about your first reiki session, it is important to understand how to act during and after the session.

What You Should Do During and After a Reiki Session

The first thing to do is to take your time researching and meeting with practitioners before you shell over your time and money to one in particular. This note has come up a lot in the book and chances are it'll come up at least a couple more times before the end. The fact of the matter is that you do not want to rush into a session with anyone. It is always best to ensure that the person in question is as certified and credible as they claim to be.

If you've been really careful about making your selection then this isn't a problem. You know you can trust the practitioner to hold up their end of the promise.

Now, it is about you and what you should be doing during the session.

To begin with, if you haven't had an interview prior to your first session then you will likely want to begin by speaking with the practitioner and informing them of any issues you may have. If you struggle with lying down or if you have issues with your lungs, anything like that should be discussed prior to beginning the session. This is good advice regardless of what you are getting reiki done for. If you are having a reiki session to help you get grounded in life then the session doesn't have anything to do with your breathing problem but that problem could come up suddenly in the session and it could cause a lot of concern. Imagine your reiki practitioner thinking they caused a breathing episode in you. That would be terrifying to them and to you. Likewise, by informing them of any and all relevant medical issues you increase your own safety because people will be prepared to handle any issues should they arise.

Reiki tends to involve light touching. Not every practitioner touches their clients but enough do in order to make it important to note. If you have problems with being touched in any particular spots then these should be pointed out to the practitioner. You could ask them to show you the hand placements they will be using, which is also a great way to see them demonstrated in action. If you aren't particularly interested in the hand motions then you could just point out to the practitioner which places bother you. Remember that you are the one in charge of what is and isn't okay when it comes to touching. Someone might not want to be touched on the side of the neck because of an injury or a sore. Another person might not want to be touched on the side of the neck simply because the feeling bothers them, not because it hurts them. Both of these reasons are perfectly valid so if you have any spots you don't want to be touched for whatever reason you absolutely must go over them with your practitioner.

One smart idea in preparing for a session is to go to the washroom prior to the session. For one, it is easier to lay down but the bigger issue is relaxation. Reiki is a very relaxing experience and one which could loosen up certain muscles. This typically isn't a problem but if you're filled up with waste then it could end up being a big problem pretty quickly.

Speaking of preparing, some people enjoy eating beforehand but then there's also people who prefer receiving reiki on an empty stomach. This is a personal choice, though I would recommend keeping yourself hydrated prior to the experience.

Most practitioners have calming music or nature sounds that they play during the session. While you are perfectly fine sticking to this soundtrack, many people like to bring in their own. Some practitioners have it set up so that they can easily play the music you desire. If this isn't an option and the music bothers you, remember that you can request it to be turned off whenever you like. A reiki practitioner wants you to be comfortable, first and foremost.

Reiki is a passive activity. You don't need to really do anything, you just let it happen to you. As you're lying there, you may find that you grow uncomfortable. Most people find that they get more comfortable the longer a session goes on but sometimes something about the prone posture can make people uncomfortable. You are allowed and encouraged to adjust your position whenever you need to. Most reiki practitioners will also have extra blankets and pillows around the room to help support you and keep you comfortable. Never be afraid to ask your reiki practitioner about things that would make the experience more comfortable.

As you leave the reiki session, there isn't a whole lot that you have to do. Most articles on reiki would tell you to simply enjoy your new peace. If you haven't eaten before your session then I definitely recommend that you do and I recommend that you continue to keep yourself hydrated. Some people report that they have no energy the night after a session but this tends to result in a deep, restful sleep and so it is one of the benefits of reiki rather than a detriment.

Where I want to push you a step further is in your mindful observation of yourself. I believe that it is a smart idea to keep a daily journal. You only need to write in it a little bit each day. It is a good way of keeping track of how you feel and what you've done differently each day. If you don't have a daily journal then you should get one before you attend reiki. Start it a couple days ahead of your first session and continue keeping it up following the session. This will help you to see with more clarity what changes reiki brings into your life. If you go back for multiple sessions then pay attention to how long the beneficial results seem to last and how much they improve your life. This step takes the most work but it is the best way to see how well reiki is working for you.

Chapter Summary

- Reiki sessions can be quite a bit different from each other. Reiki can be performed anywhere and some practitioners even do house calls. A typical session can therefore be thought of as a session you book with a practitioner that has their own practice.

- It is important to look into reiki practitioners before booking an appointment with one. Check out reviews from clients and use Google to see if the practitioner has ever been part of a scandal.

- Not every practitioner is taking on new clients, so call the practice and see if they are. If so then book your first appointment.

- Many practitioners like to have a meeting with a potential client prior to the first session. Some will book this meeting right before the first session but some like to book this meeting first and then decide whether to take on the client.

- Ask many questions when meeting your potential practitioner. They should be able to answer your questions with no problem as this is how they win your trust and show that they are trustworthy.

- Most reiki practices are designed to be inviting places with calming colors and soft music.

REIKI HEALING

- Your appointment is most likely in a quiet room with a massage table to lay on and some gentle music or nature sounds playing.

- A reiki session can be longer or shorter depending on the problems that the practitioner is trying to help you with.

- A reiki session can last anywhere from twenty to ninety minutes but most are around forty-five to sixty.

- Sometimes a reiki session can go longer than expected so don't be surprised if you have to wait longer than expected for your session.

- There is no reason to remove clothing during a reiki session and you should be suspicious of any practitioner who requests this.

- A good reiki practitioner will always ask for permission to touch you. Most will keep their hands just slightly off your body.

- Reiki practitioners should never touch you inappropriately. If one does then you should report them immediately.

- During the reiki session you may experience many different sensations. Some people feel nothing, some feel hot, others feel cold. Some report a tingling sensation. Many people report feeling like they fell asleep during the session and studies have shown that it is common for people to drop into a different state of consciousness during the process.

- Reiki is cumulative and so many people won't feel much until they've received a few sessions.

- All you need to do at your reiki session is let the practitioner do their magic but there are some things that you should share with them.

- If you have any places on your body that you don't want to or can't be touched then you should share these with your practitioner.

- If you suffer from any medical issues that make it hard for you to lay down for extended lengths of time then you should share this.

- You are free to readjust yourself for comfort at any time during the session.

- If you have music that you would prefer the practitioner to play or if you want the music turned off then you are invited to speak up.

- It is a smart idea to go to the washroom before your session.

- Some like to experience reiki on an empty stomach, others like to eat first. Consider which is best for you prior to the appointment.

- Start a journal prior to your reiki session and write in it daily. This will help you to see how you have benefited from the healing energies of the practice.

In the next chapter you will learn about the different techniques of reiki. In order to perform reiki, a person must first be attuned to the energies. This is bestowed on the student by a reiki master. You learn all about what to expect from your training in the first degree of reiki before learning the twelve hand positions for self-treatment.

CHAPTER FIVE

REIKI TECHNIQUES

Exploring reiki techniques in a book format is not particularly easy. The first issue is the fact that reiki techniques are of such a visual nature because the exact positioning of the hands is so important. We will be using a combination of photos and the written word in order to cover this. This makes this part a little bit complicated but not overly so. The second issue is the one that causes the most issue: practicing on others vs practicing on ourselves.

I don't recommend that you begin practicing reiki techniques until you have experienced a reiki session and have gotten some hands-on experience with the practice. In fact, anyone that says that they can perform reiki without this knowledge is a liar. You must seek out training with a master and open up to the first degree of training. We'll speak more about the degrees of reiki training in chapter seven so stick around for more on that. What is important now is the fact that a reiki master must first open up someone's energy in order for them to be able to channel it. This makes it literally impossible to tell you all of the techniques in play.

To tackle this problem, this chapter is going to first open up with a discussion on seeking reiki training. How do you find a reiki master who will be appropriate for you? How do you prepare yourself to take a reiki course? What should you expect from a first degree reiki course? Finally, when is it a bad idea to take a reiki course? These questions will make up the first half of this chapter as we explore the training.

While we can and should consider first degree training as a form of reiki technique, it isn't what most people are looking to hear. That is unfortunate. Most people want to jump into reiki and start using their energies to heal those around them. We aren't going to cover this deep exploration into the practice. Seek out more training and learn how to work on others from a master. What we will cover is how to perform reiki healing on ourselves. The techniques that make up the second half of this chapter are focused entirely on healing the self. This is important because the first step to healing others is to prepare ourselves. This can take months or even years depending on your relationship with the energies in question. Continue practicing with the self-healing techniques in this chapter and seek out more training before you start trying to heal others.

Let us turn our attention over to our very first training session and the achievement of the first degree of reiki.

A Crash Course On Reiki Training

The first step in reiki training is to seek out a master to learn from. We don't want to book an appointment with a con artist, neither do we want to purchase training from one. Some writings suggest that you don't find a reiki master but rather a reiki master finds you. While I appreciate what this concept is trying to get across, I think it is misguided. Each of us sets out on a path and we discover what is right for us along the way. That very well may be reiki but it is through setting out on the path of life that each of us comes to this destination.

Rather than waiting for a reiki master to approach you, go looking for one. Search online, ask your local practitioners about nearby masters or classes. Learning reiki actually isn't very hard when it comes down to it. Many people think that they are going to have to travel to Japan to learn from a reiki master but there are many of them all over North America and Europe. Finding the master is the easy part. You want to make sure, however, that the master is right for you.

I always recommend interviewing or getting to know a reiki master (or practitioner) prior to exchanging any money for their services or training. Most reiki masters will understand why you desire this and see it as a way of gaining your trust. In fact, it isn't uncommon for reiki masters to hold a meet-and-greet type session a day or two before the training begins. This allows everyone to meet each other, get comfortable with each other and see what studying reiki is all about. The master typically goes over what the training will consist of and really prepares you for the training you are going to receive.

While you are meeting with your possible master, make sure that you are asking lots of questions. Always ask lots and lots of questions. More than reviews, more than any other metric, it is through questions that con artists get ousted. Ask about the way that the course is structured. Ask about what techniques you will be covering and what techniques will still be left to learn after. Ask about how long the course will take and how much of that time is spent doing hands-on training. Make sure you also ask them about their own experiences with reiki. Ask them where they learned, how they first discovered it, who their teacher was, what type of reiki they are most proficient in. Any and all of the questions that you can think of, ask. It is always better to ask too much than to ask too little. Especially in a field such as reiki.

When preparing to take a course, keep in mind all of the real-world factors that play into making a decision like seeking training. Are you going to have to drive there? Then you'll need money for gas. Is there parking? You might need money for that. If you are going out of your way for this training, will that make it difficult for you to reach out to this master again in the future? Do you have enough to cover the cost of the training, gas, food and drink? You would hate not to consider these issues and end up having a miserable time due to them.

Reiki can be a confusing experience to those that aren't properly versed in it. I believe that it is important to have a strong relationship with your master in order to foster continued growth and development. This reiki master is going to be the one that gets you through the attunement process and this creates a deep bond between master and student. I think that students of reiki should continue to learn from their masters long after the attunement process. This doesn't mean that you should stick to local practitioners only when you are searching for a master to learn from but that you should consider the ease of communicating and visiting with your master in the future.

Book your training session now that you've found your reiki master. Let us prepare for our training.

Reiki attunement is a special, spiritual process which brings all of the energy you have from the different aspects of your life together. For many people this is the first time in their life that they will experience this coming together of all these different energies and it can be pretty difficult to go through at times. Maybe difficult isn't the best word. Challenging or overwhelming might fit better.

This overwhelming-ness of reiki attunement can be managed or even sometimes mitigated by preparing the body and mind for the training to come. Nobody has to do this in order to attend a reiki training session. These aren't hard-held rules. Instead, you should consider these preparation steps to be optional. They can help you to have the most pleasant experience possible but this isn't always the case. In fact, sometimes these tips could make the experience worse for you overall. For an example, we'll look at detoxing as a tip. There are people, myself included, that have a really hard time with this step prior to training. It might make the attunement process easier but if you are making the days before your training miserable then you are actually having a detrimental effect on the coming attunement. Only stick with those preparations which you can handle without too negative of an impact on your daily life.

The first tip is to detox yourself. It is recommended that you move to a more green style of diet prior to attunement. Rather than reaching for pig or cow, stick to meals made up of vegetables and fruit. It is recommended that these foods be raw rather than cooked. During this period you should also be drinking a lot of water. So much water. This helps you to flush out your system. Meats have a tendency to have small doses of toxins in them, or drugs from the way they were raised. Some people believe that these chemicals carry negative emotions from the animal's fear prior to ending up at your table. If you can't cut out meat entirely, cut back to just chicken or fish and make sure that you continue to drink water.

Let's revisit why it's so important to drink lots of water. This will help your body in just so many ways. One key way is that it will help to flush out toxins and detoxify your body. This is great. But we actually don't drink enough water these days. Our bodies are mostly made up of the stuff and it is incredibly important for us to refresh the supply. Water helps the body to transport nutrients to where they need to be. Basically, water helps the body to better maintain its own supply chains. Now not everyone can increase the amount of water that they are drinking. There are many medical conditions which prevent people from drinking too much water. These people cannot and should not be expected to increase their water intake prior to reiki training. For those who can, remember that an increase in water intake will mean more trips to the restroom. This might seem silly to mention but there are people who hold out from urinating, maybe they think they've taken too many breaks at work or something of the like, but this can actually lead to water poisoning and it is known to kill. So never forget, what goes in must come out.

If you are using drugs and alcohol then it is strongly recommended that you refrain from indulging in them for several days before the training. I am not here to tell you what you should or shouldn't do with your own body but it is best to come into reiki training sober, with a body that has had drugs and toxins flushed out already. This means no alcohol and no drugs.

And when I say no drugs I also mean no cigarettes or caffeine, either. This is the point where I lose a lot of people and I can understand that. I have a coffee next to me as I type these words, so I fully understand how important caffeine is to many people. While it is recommended that you avoid these substances, I would like to remind you that these are tips for preparing yourself for reiki training and they are in no way rules or requirements. If you can skip your morning coffee for a bit, that's perfect. If you can't, that's perfectly fine, too. It all depends on what you are comfortable with.

Finally, we get to the two easier aspects of preparation. Since reiki deals with emotional and spiritual energy, it is important that we don't partake in activities or practices which cause us to feel negative. Many of us love to watch the news and keep up with current events but they can be so distressing. Rather than watching the news, go out for a walk instead. Spend time doing things that fill you up with positive energy. This could be a walk, reading a book, meditating, creating art or crafts. Pretty much anything that fills you with joy is good to be partaking in right now. That is, so long as it isn't chemical joy such as drugs or alcohol.

The final step in preparation is to prepare the mind and soul. This is best achieved through meditation. Many people think that meditation means to sit in the lotus position and focus on breathing. This is one form of meditation. Did you know there are others? Have you ever given walking meditation a try? Simply go out for a walk and stay in the moment. Every time that you take a step, tell yourself, "I am taking a step." Every time the breeze cools you, bring your attention to it and tell yourself, "I am being cooled by the breeze." Basically, just go out for a walk and really stay aware of the moment. Don't go chasing the thoughts in your head, stay with your body, with the walk and the moment you are in.

Walking meditation isn't the only kind that's beneficial. Any type of meditation is. The goal here is to prepare the mind and the soul for the coming training. This is something that most people do prior to a spiritual experience. If one is about to take a pilgrimage, one considers it deeply and contemplates it ahead of time. If you are going to take a psychedelic as part of a spiritual ritual then you should take the time to meditate and contemplate it beforehand. This is exactly the same as reiki. Reiki is not a drug, nor is it a journey in the physical sense. It does represent another step, or maybe even the first step, in your spiritual journey and it should be respected as such.

With these tips out of the way, we can almost turn our attention over to the training itself. First, we should discuss the reasons that you should avoid taking a reiki course. This might seem a little odd. After all, isn't this a book about learning reiki? Why wouldn't you want to do it? Well, most of the time there is no reason not to but there are certain times when it isn't a good idea.

If you are suffering from depression or other mental illnesses which deal with the emotional realm then reiki attunement could be a very detrimental experience. Reiki sessions will help with these issues in time but the attunement process could actually make them worse and that is never an ideal outcome.

There are some illnesses and medical conditions beyond mental illness that could make reiki a bad idea. If you suffer from high blood pressure or have a pacemaker then you may want to reconsider. While there aren't many reported incidents relating to these two issues, there have been enough of them that multiple reiki practitioners I interviewed have brought them up. Another issue that comes up is epilepsy. Reiki attunement doesn't necessarily have anything to do with these conditions but the experience can raise the blood pressure or heart-rate of the individual who is undergoing the attunement. With epilepsy the problem isn't the heart-rate as much as the fact that many people report seeing colors or bright lights during the attunement process. These are stressors for epilepsy and it may be best to avoid reiki if you suffer from this illness.

Another issue that people worry about is how reiki attunement will interact with their medications. If you need medication to live then you probably really want that medication present in your body. The reiki attunement process is said to cleanse the body of toxins and people worry that this will result in their medications being flushed out by reiki. There is no sign of this affecting people's medications. It could be that reiki doesn't really detoxify the body on a physical level. Or, it could be that as a compassionate and healing process, reiki serves to increase the healthiness of the individual and therefore it doesn't interfere with those chemicals which are working to help the body to function properly.

One of the elements which you must consider for yourself is whether or not you want to take a reiki training course while pregnant. I could not find any reports of problems with pregnant women and the reiki attunement process and the masters I interviewed all reported having trained pregnant women in the past. One was training a pregnant woman the weekend after we spoke and they had no concerns about her health or the health of the baby. The problem with pregnancy isn't anything medical but simply how much energy it takes to do the courses. This being physical energy, not spiritual. If you are exhausted or having troubles sitting or lying down for long periods of time then I would recommend waiting until after you've had the baby to sign up for classes.

You are still here and still ready for your reiki training course! Let us look at what can be expected here. Afterwards we will turn our attention over to using our newfound reiki skills to perform reiki techniques on ourselves.

Most reiki training courses are carried out over several days. The first degree, the easiest and lowest level of reiki, is taught over the course of two to four days. Most reiki masters like to teach the first level using four classes. These can be split between two days or four, it really depends on how intense the training sessions are to be. There is about twelve to fifteen hours of study and training to unlock the first degree of reiki.

Many training courses begin with the history of reiki, so you've already got that part down through this book. There aren't typically any tests on the history of reiki but if there were then you'd be set to ace them. The training moves from history lessons into technique and shows the hand positions for both self-treatment and treatment of others. All of this is sprinkled in with stories of past experiences, lessons learned from other masters and tips for how to best use reiki for healing. Much of this is broken up with partnered practice for some hands-on experience.

One thing that is often quite common in reiki courses is a lack of paper and note-taking. Most people think, of course, about learning as a child and all the homework they had to do but reiki is often taught as an oral tradition. This means that the knowledge and teachings come from the mouth of the master and into the ears of the students. Those students, if they were to become masters, would then be expected to continue the tradition by keeping their teaching oral. This is one of the reasons why a book on reiki pales in comparison to experiencing it yourself and taking a course.

For an example of a typical reiki course, let us use a weekend. Many people can only train on the weekends since they work the 9-to-5 lifestyle. Weekend courses tend to start on Friday rather than Saturday with the Friday sessions being short introductions. This is typically done in the evening and only takes a couple of hours at most. It is for the students to meet the master, meet each other and learn what they're in for.

REIKI HEALING

Saturday is where things start to get real. Unlike Friday, this will be a long session. Both Saturday and Sunday will be full days. Saturday will likely begin with another meeting session. This is for anyone that missed the previous evening's introduction. As the day continues, the topics will focus entirely on reiki and how it works, how people can start to get involved in it, the benefits it has. Discussion about the four attunements will be of extreme interest. Saturday is when most masters give their students the first level of attunement. During this the principles of reiki, how important it is to keep up the practice and stay healthy and how to further your spiritual training are typically brought up. The second level of attunement is given near the end of the day.

Saturday typically has a bit of reiki practice but this is most often left for Sunday. Sunday sees the students receive the third and fourth level of attunement from the master. The third is often near the start of the day, the fourth early in the afternoon. There is a focus on the hand positions and how to use the healing energy of reiki to the best of your ability. Students practice partnering up with other learners and practicing on each other. Discussions about ways that reiki can improve your life and how you can use it in your day-to-day life will also feature highly.

This brings most reiki courses to a conclusion. There are some masters, however, who prefer to teach much more involved courses. Some masters believe that reiki should be one part of a spiritual practice and so they also teach skills like meditation and mindfulness and visualization. These courses could end up being a lot longer than the typical training session but they are the outliers. For the most part, you can expect to learn the first degree of reiki over the course of the weekend.

Healing Yourself With Reiki

Self-treatment with reiki requires you to listen to your body. Each of us has a body that talks to us but we often don't listen. Mostly the problem is that we don't understand the language of the body. We've taken an introductory course, so to speak, so we each know that being tired means we need sleep and our stomach rumbling means that we are hungry. What about the other signals? Do you know what tension means in your muscles? How about behind your eyes? There are all sorts of ways our body tries to tell us what it needs and the first technique you need to master to heal yourself with reiki is to learn to listen.

The good news with this lesson is that you don't need to have taken your reiki course yet to start working this into your lifestyle. Reiki can help us to understand our bodies better but it isn't necessary. This understanding is important if we want our self-directed reiki sessions to go well but reiki isn't important to achieve the understanding. To keep with the language metaphor, learning to listen to your body is like learning to read while reiki is akin to writing poetry. Learning about your body and how it communicates with you is something that I recommend everyone does. Even if you finish this book and decide that reiki isn't for you, please, I beg you, learn to listen to your body. This one change will improve your life overall.

The first degree of reiki focuses on self-healing, so if you want to practice reiki on yourself properly then you are going to need to have taken the training and been attuned to the energies necessary for reiki to work in the first place. If you have this training then you will already have gone through many, if not all, of the following hand positions but it is always useful to have an easy-to-consult guide. Self-healing with reiki focuses on improving the way your energy flows through your body and it can really help you to remove those negative blockages that impact your quality of life.

Don't forget that there is a psychological component to reiki. We heal our brains and souls through this process. Past events and struggles that have left an impact on you are prone to re-emerge. This part of the process can be quite painful for some people, especially those who have dealt with trauma when they were younger such as abuse or the loss of a parent. Trauma from when we are young is often the most vulnerable and painful. I have met people who have not been able to stick with a program of reiki or meditation due to the way past pains assailed their mind. The sad thing about this is that through meditation and reiki we can actually overcome this type of pain but it requires us to face our fears and be brave. If you are worried about what might surface in your mind then approach reiki carefully. Rather than just starting a session maybe it is best if you reflect on your trauma ahead of time and work on overcoming it in your mind. Or, at the very least, rather than overcoming it might be best to focus simply on being able to sit with it. If you can sit with your pain, with your discomfort, then you will find that over time it grows less painful, it seems to shrink. Reiki can help to speed up this shrinkage but you must first be willing to face the issues that trouble you.

You will learn in your reiki training course that practitioners use an invocation to begin. This is simply just a meaningful phrase you say to help you set your intention. You need to have the intention of using reiki and this requires you to be in the right state of mind. An invocation is a way of invoking your chosen state of mind. Most people eventually create their own but it can be as simple as, "I allow the healing energies of reiki to flow through me." Reiki will sometimes flow without an invocation, because that is what reiki does. It is constantly in a state of flow around us. The invocation helps us to tap into it. If reiki is a river then the invocation is like a water wheel that allows us to tap into the unlimited healing energy flowing around us all the time.

Reiki energy isn't uniform, however, and we don't really control it. While it might be nice to think of what we do as shaping the reiki energy, this wouldn't be correct. Reiki energy has a "mind" of its own. You might be planning to heal an emotional pain, say the pain from a recent romantic breakup, but the reiki might affect a different area, such as a deeper rooted pain from your past. Often these line-up in a way that we didn't expect. That deep-rooted pain from your past could very well be the thing that has caused you stress and problems in the romantic relationship. So rather than healing the pain you intended to, the reiki heals the true source of the pain.

When you first begin to practice reiki you must stick to healing yourself. You need to create the room inside of yourself to open yourself up to further training before you can start to heal others. The first degree of reiki is all about self-improvement rather than outward healing. One of the big problems we have in improving ourselves is a lack of understanding or grounding when it comes to the self. We might think that we need to improve one area of our life but be completely oblivious to the deeper problems that are truly keeping us from achieving greatness or happiness. The goal with the first degree of reiki is to heal yourself by letting the healing energies of reiki fill you up to increase your awareness of yourself, your emotions, your pains and your behaviors. Many people describe the effect that self-directed reiki has on their lives as a form of cleaning. It is as if you finally opened up all the shutters on that old house, let the air blow through and started tossing old and useless materials to the curb. Of course those materials are thoughts, feelings and pains that you have been carrying with you throughout your daily life.

The way to get the most out of the first degree of reiki is to use reiki on yourself on a daily basis. This becomes a part of a self-care routine that will greatly heal you. By practicing every day, you are going to be able to see a much faster and larger improvement in your wellbeing. Have you ever let your dishes go a few days without washing them? If you have then you know how quickly they pile up. When there's a lot of dishes, it takes a long time to clean them. If you wash them after every meal then you only ever need to clean a little bit and you can relax with the time you saved or you can use it to clean the kitchen and keep the whole place looking great. Reiki is similar. When we let days go by without practicing on ourselves we lose a little bit of the progress we made. Then we need to commit even more time to our healing. When we practice everyday, we keep our bodies clean and functioning great.

There are twelve key hand positions that are used for self-healing. Understanding the healing of these hand positions can be a little confusing to beginners. They think that you must cover the exact area you want to heal with your hands but that isn't always the case. Reiki is that it is an energy that flows through us, that moves through our bodies. Any reiki healing that you undergo is, by definition, a healing that affects your whole body. The hand positions do offer more value than this, otherwise there would be no need for hand positions at all. Each hand position is chosen carefully for where the energy enters and which part of the body it moves through first. Think of it like heating a house. The whole house heats up when you crank up the temperature but the places which get warmest are those where the radiators are. The hand positions are like radiators, they direct the most energy in the area they are placed but this energy then continues throughout the whole body.

Each hand position should be held or kept for about five minutes or so, which means that treating yourself will take about an hour. You could shrink this down to about half an hour but anything less than that and there is almost no point. While you can shrink it, I am going to recommend that you don't. An hour might be a lot of time in a busy life but it is time you use to take care of yourself and we could all learn to tend to ourselves a little more.

Let's take a look at those twelve hand positions.

Reiki Hand Positions

We begin our hand positions from the top of the body and work our way down. First from the front, then from the back. There is no reason for you to follow the outline given here; it's a guide. Start with whichever position you want to and switch to whichever position you feel should follow. The goal here is not to hit them in order but rather simply to make sure that you use each of them during your sessions.

REIKI HEALING

#1: The first position is the back of the head. Lift your arms over your head and place your palms on the back of your skull. Your fingers should meet in the middle of the back of your head and they should appear to mostly be pointed down. This is one of the positions which works on the brain. Since the brain contains the central nervous system, the ears, the eyes, nose, mouth, pineal gland and the endocrine system, this makes this an extremely important position. That said, hand position #2 and #3 both also focus on these areas.

#2: Cover your eyes with your hands. Pretend like you are playing peekaboo with a baby but leave your hands over your eyes for the full five minutes. Your hands should only touch each other at the end of your pinky fingers. To achieve this, keep your palms over your eyes and use your nose as a separator between your hands. If you were to flip your hands around then you would see they create a V-shape. Your fingers should be resting on your forehead and pointing inwards towards each other.

#3: This time the focus is on the ears rather than the eyes. This reiki position is a bit different from how most people cover their ears. When told to cover their ears most people place their palms over their ears in a horizontal position so that their thumbs rest on or under the earlobe and their elbows are pointed out in front of them. We want to use a vertical position for reiki. Your elbows should be pointed down and your hands covering your ears from the bottom to the top. This will result in the heel of your palms being placed just under the earlobe. Make sure that you keep your fingers pointed upwards rather than curling them around the top of the ear.

#4: Now it is time to move down to our throats. Place your left hand on the right side of your neck. Your right hand will then cross over your left hand to hold the left side of your neck. The crossing of your hands is important here but which hand is first and which is second doesn't matter. Your elbows should be pointed at the ground. Your fingers will be pointed upwards at a very slight angle but more important is the fact that they'll also be pointed behind you. With position #3, we don't curl our fingers around our ears but with this position we do slightly wrap them around the neck. This position focuses the most attention on the neck, throat and thyroid. Since it is also quite high on the body, your eyes, ears and mouth will all see an increased benefit from this position.

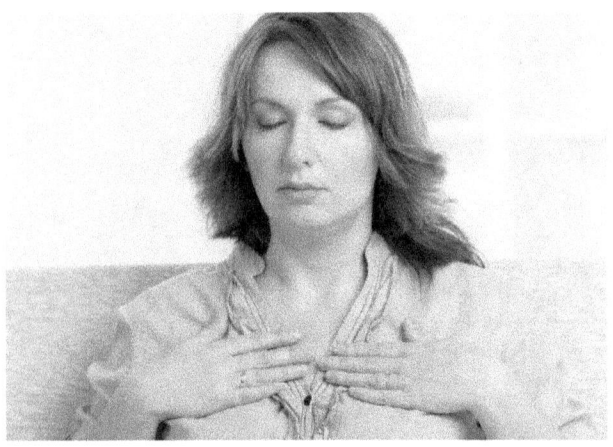

#5: This position is extremely important because it works on your heart and lungs and all of the important vital organs in your upper body. Place one hand over the center of your chest diagonally. Left hand on the right side, right hand on the left side. Your palms will cover each other to direct all of your energy towards the same central position. Your fingers will be pointed upwards but slightly outwards to each side. A good way to ensure that you get this position right is to line up your index fingers with your collarbone.

#6: This position gives those lower parts of your torso extra attention. Lower means that it focuses on your liver, small intestine, stomach, spleen, gallbladder and the muscles. Modern science has shown that our stomachs have plenty of neurons in them (the thinking part of your brain), which is why we trust our gut feelings. If you are looking to heal your mind with reiki then don't neglect your stomach. With your elbows out to your sides but bent, place your hands underneath your breasts (or where they would be, men). The fingers of each hand point towards each other with your middle fingers just barely touching.

#7: This position is even lower on the torso and it focuses on the kidneys, the digestive system, the urinary tract and the reproductive organs. Do the exact same hand position as #6 but keep it over the stomach rather than just below the breasts. Your hands should curve slightly around the sides of your body.

#8: The last of the hand positions for the front of the body, this one is easiest to do when you are kneeling down. Place your hands on the side of your body. This position is said to help with the bones in the body and the other components like skin and blood. The biggest benefits of this position are in the large intestine, the pelvis, hips and legs and the waste system of the body. Your hands should slightly curve around the sides of your body but, instead of pointing at each other, they point in and downwards. The fingers on your left hand should be pointed towards your right leg and vise versa.

#9: Moving to the back, this position helps your shoulders and the muscles around the neck. Place each palm over a shoulder, your arms crossing in the middle. If done correctly then your arms should cross just above your chest. Each hand curves around the shoulder so that the fingers of your hand are pointing down your back.

#10: This position is like a reflection of #6 but for your back rather than your front. It is used for directing healing energies into the upper back, heart and lungs. Reach your arms behind your back so that your palms rest just slightly below your shoulder blades. Your elbows should be out to the side and your fingers should be pointed towards each other with the middle fighters just barely touching at the tips.

#11: This one is best done while sitting down. Place your arms even lower on your back, just above your waist. This is done to heal the middle part of your back and the organs in this area like your liver, kidneys and spleen. Your fingers should be pointed towards each other and the middle fingers should just barely be touching at the tips. Your elbows will still be pointed out from your body but with more of a downward slant than a horizontal one as position #10 demands.

#12: The final position is the buttocks. While sitting down, reach your arms behind you and under your butt. Your arms will be mostly straight down at your sides but with a slight curve to the elbows. Your fingers should be pointed slightly inwards towards the center of your body and you can curve them around if there is room to do so comfortably. This position is for healing the lower back, your intestines, bladder and colon.

Chapter Summary

- You must seek out a reiki master in order to be trained in the art. Make sure you research and check out any master prior to giving them your money.

- It is a good idea to interview a master ahead of time if you can. Many masters have open meetings with students prior to classes. This allows them to meet you, you to meet them and they can use the time to make sure you understand what reiki is and what reiki isn't.

- Reiki attunement is a four step process that happens over the course of about two full days of training.

- It is recommended that you detox before your training.

- Drink lots of water to flush your system ahead of time.

- Abstain from drugs and alcohol beforehand. Also avoid caffeine and nicotine if you are able to without too many detrimental effects.

- Avoid situations that cause you emotional pain beforehand and meditate.

- Those suffering from depression might find the attunement process to be a negative one and it may be best to wait until you aren't so depressed to take the training.

- Some illnesses and medical conditions may have problems with the attunement process.

- The first day of a reiki training session will cover the first two attunements and theory. The second day will cover the two remaining attunements and focus on hands-on training.

- The first degree of reiki is best used for healing yourself. You can technically use it on friends and family but you should have a solid grounding in self-treatment before you start working on others.

- Most practitioners use an invocation to begin the reiki healing.

- Reiki energy is not uniform and so sometimes it ebbs and flows.

- Use reiki on yourself on a daily basis. This will see an improvement in your life as well as increase your confidence in your ability.

- There are twelve key hand positions for self-treatment. Each should be held for five minutes, making for a sixty minute session.

- The first hand position is the back of the head and it helps to heal the brain and the senses.

REIKI HEALING

- The second position covers the eyes and it helps heal the brain and the senses, too.

- The third position covers the ears and it helps heal the same way as the previous two.

- These first three hand positions all primarily heal the same places. This is because while reiki flows through your whole body it is strongest at the source. The third position is thus better for dealing with ear pain but it will help with eye pain, too, and even pain in your legs or feet.

- The fourth position is around the throat and it is used to heal the voice, the neck, your mouth and thyroid.

- The fifth position is over the center of the chest and it helps with the heart and lungs.

- The sixth position is below the breasts and it is good for healing the stomach, spleen, small intestine, muscles, gallbladder and liver.

- The seven position is just a little lower than the sixth and it helps with the stomach, kidneys, digestive system, reproductive organs and urinary tract.

- The eighth position is on the sides of the lower torso and it helps with healing the large intestine, pelvis, hips, legs and waste system.

- The ninth position is the shoulders and helps to reduce pain in this area.

- The tenth position is on the upper back and it helps to heal the heart, lungs and upper back.

- The eleventh position is the lower back and is used to heal the liver, kidneys, spleen and lower back pain.

- The twelve and final position for self-treatment is on the buttocks and it helps to heal the lower back, intestines, bladder and colon.

In the next chapter you will learn how reiki can be used to treat your headaches, backaches, arthritis, high blood pressure and eczema. There are more issues that reiki can be used to treat, of course, so don't worry if your particular issue isn't addressed. There are plenty of resources online that will help you tackle it!

CHAPTER SIX

REIKI FOR COMMON AILMENTS

While some people try to convince others that reiki can be used to heal anything, this isn't true. Reiki can be a great source of relief from the ailments listed in this chapter. It is important to understand the limitations of reiki, yes, and it is just as important to spend time looking at the practical applications of this practice.

We're going to spend this chapter looking at how reiki can help with headaches, backaches, arthritis, high blood pressure and eczema.

Headaches

Headaches are one of the pains that reiki is best at treating. Remember that headaches are caused for a reason. The most common reason is that you weren't drinking enough water and your brain is swelling but that is merely one possibility. There are many reasons why you might get a headache and medical care should be considered if you find that you are having them often all of a sudden.

We all get headaches now and then and reiki is great to treat this. In the last chapter we looked at three different hand positions all around the head. The first position is the best for dealing with a headache. I suggest laying down for this one and spending no less than five minutes in the position. If the headache still persists after ten minutes then try changing your position to one of the other head-centered positions we explored.

Surprisingly, however, a headache could often be caused by an energy blockage, in which case the best choice is to treat the feet rather than the head. The goal with this is to break up the blockage from the lowest part of the body. Spend five minutes on your feet and then move up your legs and into the stomach positions and continue moving upwards from there until the headache subsides.

Backaches

Before treating your back pain you must realize that the source of your back pain could still persist after a reiki session. For example, if you are experiencing back pain and you also lift heavy objects for a living then even if you relieve your back pain with reiki for the night you are still going to be exposing yourself to more pain once you return to work. Reiki can't change the way you act or treat your back, it can only address the pain that has been caused. If you don't lift or have a bad posture but are suffering a backache then this could be an energy blockage and reiki could help a lot.

We explored a handful of reiki techniques for treating the back. Start by selecting the one that is closest to the area of your pain and hold the position for five to ten minutes. If this is uncomfortable, or if it fails to relieve your backache, then you may need to start with a slightly different position (either higher or lower on your back) and work your way towards the painful area.

Arthritis

Arthritis is one of those pains which reiki won't fully heal but it will greatly reduce the amount of pain and discomfort it causes. Since arthritis can be found pretty much anywhere on the human body, it is hard to recommend a particular hand position for treating it. Pick the hand position that is closest to the pain and hold it for fifteen minutes at least once a day, twice a day if it is particularly painful.

Trying to deal with arthritis can be a very stressful and frustrating experience. Trust me, I know. It runs in my family and I have seen the detrimental effects it can have on a person. While we use reiki healing to treat our headaches and backaches when we have them, arthritis (and other similar issues like carpal tunnel syndrome) should be treated through daily reiki applications. Even if you don't feel arthritis pain on a given day, don't skip a session. It is important to keep up and fight against your arthritis, as skipping a day will let it gain more ground against you and it commonly leads to energy blockages.

High Blood Pressure

There is no position which helps in lowering your blood pressure. If I had to pick an area, I would say to focus on the torso. This is an effect, however, that we see happen through the use of reiki regardless of where on the body the practitioner positions their hands. This is because most high blood pressure is caused through stress and poor living. Reiki greatly reduces stress and it promotes healthier living. The reduction in stress can see an immediate effect on blood pressure but the other requires longer.

As you work through reiki healing you will find that you naturally start to take better care of yourself. You begin listening to your body better and you respect your body, mind, spirit and self much more as the energy of reiki accumulates in your body. This results in a reduction of blood pressure due to diet, lack of exercise and the like.

Eczema

Eczema is a skin condition that can be quite irritating to live with. It typically isn't associated with life-threatening issues but it lowers the quality of life for the person suffering from it. Eczema causes the skin to become inflamed and it can crack, often turn red and it itches. It can also cause blisters and these can range from annoying to extremely painful.

Eczema should be treated with a combination of modern medicine and reiki healing. Reiki sessions should be often, daily if possible, as this is one of those issues that doesn't arise and disappear like headaches. It takes daily commitment to beat it. Use hand position #8 and #12 from the previous chapter for treating eczema. These are the lowest positions in the front and the back and they are used for treating the groin and bowels, as well as the skin, blood and bones.

REIKI HEALING

Chapter Summary

- Reiki shouldn't be used exclusively to heal major medical issues. It is always best to combine reiki with modern medicine.

- Headaches are often caused by underlying issues but reiki can be a good way to reduce the pain they cause you.

- Use a position around your head to heal a headache. If this doesn't work then start from your feet and work your way up your body to remove any blockages which might be causing the pain.

- Reiki often can't treat the underlying reason that you have a backache, such as when you overextend yourself physically, but it can reduce the pain.

- Use one of the positions for treating the back, upper or lower depending on where the pain is. If the pain is too great to reach the sore spot then start above or below it and slowly work your way towards it.

- Arthritis is another issue that can't be entirely cured with reiki but it will help to reduce the pain and discomfort.

- Since arthritis can affect pretty much any area in the body it will be up to you to pick the position that is best for you.

- When treating arthritis with reiki it is best to have a daily reiki session. Increase this to twice daily if the pain is more severe.

- Reiki's positive benefits accumulate in the body and so it is important to remember your treatments everyday.

- High blood pressure tends to be caused by other issues in life such as stress and diet. Reiki is fantastic at treating stress which will then help to lower high blood pressure.

- Those who get into reiki have a tendency to start living a healthier, happier life afterwards. This results in more exercise, relaxation and better dieting habits and all of these can help to reduce high blood pressure.

- Eczema is a skin condition that can cause a lot of pain. It is best treated with a combination of reiki and modern medicine.

- To treat eczema use both the lower front and lower back positions as these help with skin, blood and bone.

In the next chapter you will learn all about the three degrees of reiki from shoden, the first, through to shinpiden, the third. This book has focused on the first degree but I encourage you to continue your learning and progress through the remaining degrees.

CHAPTER SEVEN

THE THREE DEGREES OF REIKI

We've briefly mentioned the three degrees of reiki throughout the book but our focus has been on the first degree. This is because the first degree is the one that beginners to reiki must achieve and then work through in order to reach the others. A beginner is not going to be able to get to the second or third degrees without first progressing the self-healing of the first degree.

It is worth learning about the three degrees before we finish our time together. These are Shoden, the first degree; Okuden, the second degree; and Shinpiden, the third degree and, having completed, the one at which you are said to be a master. Let us take a look at each of these in turn.

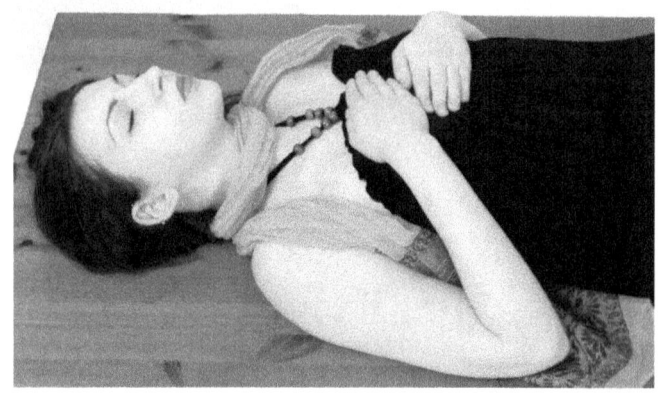

First Degree - Shoden

The first degree of reiki is the easiest. It can be learned from a master in a couple of days. This is considered to be a gentle version of reiki. This is good because when it comes to working with energies, we want to start gentle and slow rather than diving into the deep end. The first degree of reiki requires the student to go through four different attunements in order to open them up to the energy so that they can channel it through themselves.

There are some people that suggest using the first degree of reiki on friends and family members. While this is something that you can do, I personally believe it is better to focus on the self. You want to learn how these energies work, how they feel, how you can open yourself up to them the best. This will make you better at performing reiki but it also means that you take more time for yourself and thus you will find that your own life improves through the process.

This stage of reiki is quite tame and there isn't much more we can say about it that we haven't covered already. It is the stage at which an individual can transition from receiving reiki sessions to using reiki on themselves at home.

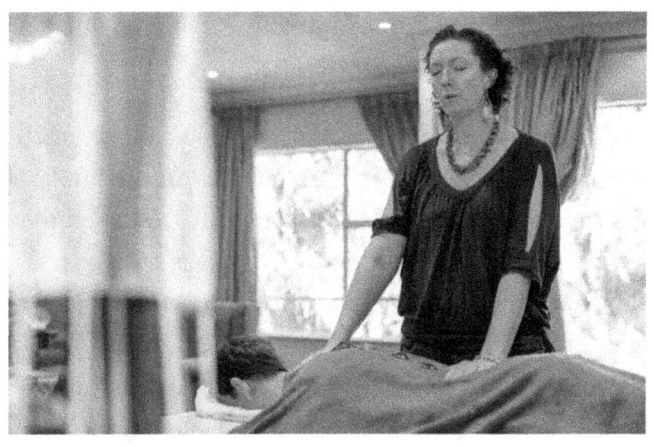

Second Degree - Okuden

The second degree of reiki has two more attunements which must be given from a master. This opens up the individual to higher levels of vibrational energy and allows them to start using these energies to better the lives of others. It is at this stage that the practitioner is ready to start using reiki to heal others rather than themselves. It is also at this level that I believe a practitioner is ready to start treating their friends and family.

Symbols are brought in with this level and these help with centering the mind to open the practitioner up to a better control of the reiki energy. It is also in this stage that the master will start to teach the practitioner about how to scan a person's body to feel how their energy is flowing and find any blockages they are suffering from.

The second degree of reiki is the stage at which the practitioner is ready to start practicing on the public. It is considered to be the level at which the practitioner becomes a professional. Because of this, it is often paired with business teachings in North America. These cover issues like starting your own reiki business, how to interview clients and professionally inquire about their medical history. It also has a strong focus on listening to the client to hear both what they are saying and what is under what they are saying. This allows the practitioner to more readily target the problem areas in the client's energies. Classes also tend to discuss other business issues such as insurance, finding clients, and dealing with the legal paperwork necessary for a practice.

Third Degree - Shinpiden

The third degree of reiki marks the path to becoming a master. While the first and second degrees are often taught in classes over one period of time, the third degree is taught in two halves. The first half sees them becoming a master as they are attuned to the highest level of reiki. The second half of the third degree focuses on how to be a teacher of reiki. We'll focus on the first half of this, as the second half concentrates on much deeper issues than we can get into here such as taking on clients and how to attune others.

REIKI HEALING

The reiki master is opened up to a deep and rich level of vibration which greatly improves the quality of their reiki. Since they are more readily able to use all of the energy of reiki, rather than just a little, this makes them powerful masters of energy. The master symbols are taught at this point, which are what masters use to attune others. These symbols are only given when the master commits to the second half of the third degree.

Achieving the third degree of reiki takes a lot of work. While the first degree can be learned by just about anybody that is willing, the third degree takes extensive effort and learning. It should be obvious that one doesn't become a master without first committing to the training. It is no surprise to learn that you need to spend a great amount of time working the energies of reiki to become a master. What does surprise people is how important their own health is to their training journey. A master is expected to understand and practice meditation and mindfulness and to live a life that promotes healthy living through diet, exercise and mental/spiritual self care.

Chapter Summary

- There are three degrees of reiki: Shoden, Okuden and Shinpiden.

- The first degree can be trained in two days. The student goes through four attunements with a master and is guided in how to use reiki for self-healing and minor healing of others.

- I recommend spending your time practicing on yourself first before you start using your new-found reiki abilities on your friends and family.

- The second degree requires two more attunements. At the second degree you are considered to be a practitioner and so much of the coursework for this level involves learning how to open a practice, find clients and deal with the legal issues of practicing reiki healing.

- The third degree is for masters. It is taught in two different parts. The first part teaches the student to be a master by attuning them to the highest level of reiki, the second half teaches the master how to teach reiki and work students through the attunement process.

- It takes a lot of work, both with reiki and with self-care and spiritual growth, in order to reach the level of a reiki master.

FINAL WORDS

I wish I could tell you that you now know everything you need to know about reiki but that isn't even close to true. We have focused on Usui reiki but there are other reiki styles that could be explored and elaborated on. We focused on an introduction to reiki and a brief look at the self-healing powers of the first degree plus there are two more degrees to study and master in reiki. This book could only take you so far. To truly master this practice, you need practical, hands-on experience.

Rather than recap the book that you have just finished, I would like to take this time to point you towards further learning. If you are truly interested in pursuing reiki, then where do you go from here?

The first step is to get your first degree attunement through a master. Chapter Five described what a training session is like but this does not replace the need to experience the class. A book like this can give you introductory knowledge but it does not have the power to attune you to the energies of reiki. That would be incredible, but also incredibly dangerous. Instead, make sure that you seek out an expert and learn from them. As far as where to go next, it is always best to ask your teacher and work with them. They will understand you and your energies and their suggestions for training and expansion of skill will be invaluable.

One of the things that I think anyone who wants to take reiki seriously should do is visit Japan. This is an expensive suggestion, I realize, but one that I think will provide you with great benefits. In Japan, you will be able to track down masters of incredible skill, especially those who stick most closely to Usui's original teachings. There is so much knowledge to be gained from these masters that you could spend the rest of your life soaking up the knowledge they have.

For many people, there isn't anywhere else to go. Getting your attunement will allow you to practice reiki on yourself and this is more than enough for most. Honestly, I can't blame them. Most of us don't want to heal others. Well, we do but we don't want to go through the struggles of learning and setting up a practice and we're (rightfully) wary about the harm we could accidentally cause someone should we mislead them. Plus reiki can bring up a lot of painful memories and many don't know how to deal with another's pain well.

Yet self-treatment is much easier and simple. You don't need to worry about hurting another and you get to improve your life in a massive way. What isn't to love about that? If someone came to you and said, "I have a way of improving your life, it costs almost nothing at all and you can take it with you no matter where you go," it would be negligent not to listen and give it a try.

So what are you waiting for? Go book an appointment and get attuned to the first degree of reiki.

www.ingramcontent.com/pod-product-compliance
Lightning Source LLC
Chambersburg PA
CBHW050321120526
44592CB00014B/2002